INSECT MUSICIANS
& CRICKET CHAMPIONS

INSECT MUSICIANS

&

CRICKET CHAMPIONS

A Cultural History of
Singing Insects
in China and Japan

Lisa Gail Ryan

CHINA BOOKS & PERIODICALS, INC.

SAN FRANCISCO

China Books & Periodicals, Inc.
2929 24th Street
San Francisco, CA 94110

Insect-Musicians and Cricket Champions of China by Berthold Laufer. Published 1927 by The Field Museum of Natural History.

"Insect-Musicians" from *Exotics and Retrospectives* by Lafcadio Hearn. Published 1898 by Little, Brown and Company.

Quote from *The Mustard Seed Garden Manual of Painting*, in *The Tao of Painting: A Study of the Ritual Disposition of Chinese Painting*, courtesy of Princeton University Press.

Book and jacket design by Linda Revel

Photo Credits:
ChinaStock, L' Image Odier-Danee Hazama, Clint Shaw

Cover Photo by Clint Shaw

Insect cages and paraphernalia courtesy of the Ryan family

Every effort has been made to find copyright holders for the material in this book. We apologize for any unintentional omissions. We would be happy to insert acknowledgments in any subsequent edition.

Library of Congress Catalog Card Number: 95-83935

ISBN 0-8351-2576-9

First Edition

10 9 8 7 6 5 4 3 2 1

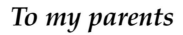

To my parents

If the moonlight could be heard
it would sound
like the song of a cricket.

— CAROL HAMMOND

CONTENTS

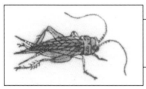

PREFACE

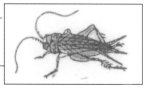

BERTHOLD LAUFER was a curator of anthropology at the Field Museum of Natural History in Chicago.

He wrote *Insect-Musicians and Cricket Champions of China* when he returned from the 1923 Captain Marshall Field Expedition to China. On the trip he collected more than two hundred and forty insect cages, cricket jars, dishes, ticklers and other related items for the museum. *Insect-Musicians and Cricket Champions of China* was intended to give a brief introduction to the collection of cricket paraphernalia on exhibit.

The original text has been included in its entirety with the exception of references to specific items that were on display in the museum at the time the text was written in 1927. Eleven of the twelve plates, originally produced in photogravure, have been included. The plates with their captions have been reproduced in a brown tint to capture the spirit of the original photographs. The plate numbers have been altered to accommodate the deletion of the missing plate. New full-color photographs have been added throughout.

The layout of the essay has been retained with the exception of long excerpts which have been set in block quotations. Current scientific research and author's notes appear in the margins in tinted boxes or in brackets within the text where necessary. Chapter divisions have also been added to incorporate the new information and illustrations. The original transliterations of Chinese have been left unchanged. Chinese translations appearing in the author's notes are in *pinyin*.

"Insect-Musicians" was written in 1898 by Lafcadio Hearn. Hearn was perhaps one of the best known expatriates living in Japan during that time. He was a professor at the Imperial University of Tokyo and a prolific writer. "Insect-Musicians" originally appeared in his book entitled *Exotics and Retrospectives* published by Little, Brown and Company. It has been included in its entirety and the original layout has been kept where possible. All of the line drawings from the book are included in the text and are used to illustrate the end papers of this book. The footnotes have been moved to the end of the essay, with the exception of the prices of insects which have been listed under the text for clarity.

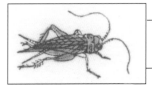 # ACKNOWLEDGMENTS

Grateful acknowledgment is made to the following people:

Russ Bassett of Bassett's Cricket Ranch for providing information about cricket breeding; William W. Cade of Brock University for his insight into the world of cricket sounds; Jack Catlin for his kindness and enthusiasm, and for loaning me some of the cricket cages pictured in this book; Ma Baolin for proofreading the *pinyin*; Wendy Lee for providing Chinese characters; Chris Noyes and Greg Jones for their confidence in this project; Gary Clark for his advice; Dennis Cox of ChinaStock Photo Library for tracking down the photos from China; Patsy Lee Donegan for her suggestions; Jamie Draluck for patience; Cassie Jones and Kim Smashey, my editors, for their flexibility and hard work; Pierre of L'Image Odier for his generosity and exceptional photographs; Gary Pahl of San Francisco State University for his comments on the ancient history sections; Linda Revel for her perseverance, understanding of my unconventional working style and for burning the midnight oil; Clint Shaw for his encouragement, patience with uncooperative crickets and beautiful photographs; Karen Makal and Linda and Peter Lindberg of the Gourd Factory for sharing their knowledge about gourd growing. I also wish to acknowledge the Field Museum of Natural History in Chicago; Little, Brown and Company; and Jin Xing-Bao and Raymond Nagai for providing the lists of insects in the appendix.

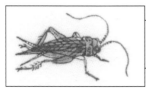

INTRODUCTION

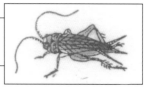

FOSSIL EVIDENCE TELLS US that insects first appeared about four hundred million years ago. Some scientists estimate that there are ten quintillion insects on the planet earth, roughly eighty percent of the world's species. They are found in almost every climate, on every continent, and in every culture. The Athenians pictured them on their coins, painted them on their ceramics, and wore insect jewelry in their hair. The Northern Europeans believed that grasshoppers had medicinal qualities that made warts disappear, and Mexican children glue rhinestones on beetles' backs and keep them as pets. While many cultures have been interested in insects, few have been so fascinated by them as the people of Asia.

The Chinese began to keep pet insects as early as the Táng dynasty (A.D. 618-906). In Japan there are records of insect hunts dating back to A.D. 1095. Of all the insects, the cricket has intrigued the people of Asia like no other insect. Artists, scholars, backyard scientists, emperors and peasants have been enamored of the cricket for more than a thousand years. They are the subject of art, literature, mythology, music, and gambling matches. They have become totems, medicines, symbols, and pets. Crickets in Asia have a rich and significant social history. They are an integral part of Asia's identity.

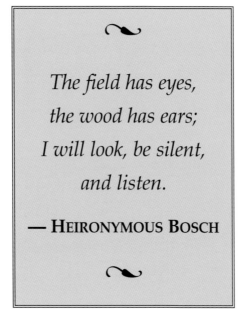

The field has eyes,
the wood has ears;
I will look, be silent,
and listen.

— HEIRONYMOUS BOSCH

This passion for crickets has given rise to a unique pastime like no other. By the Sung dynasty (A.D. 960-1278) in China, crickets were a popular topic of discussion at teashops and street markets. Fashionable people were never without chirping crickets concealed under their robes. The Japanese celebrated the chirping song of the cricket in poetry and legend and evening insect hunts were a popular pastime.

But, by early this century the popularity of insect keeping waned. In China, some said it was a "petty diversion".

Today, in China and Japan, the interest in insects is being revived. Antique cages are avidly sought after by collectors, and the art of breeding crickets is back in style. In China, crickets are sold at the street markets again. The Tama Zoo, just outside Tokyo, holds an annual autumn insect show and department stores sell electronic chirping bugs and recorded cricket music.

In the following pages, the cricket exhibits his undeniable charm. By day he is silent but when darkness falls, he sings in a tiny, delicate voice that reminds us of the universal connection of all people to the natural world.

PART ONE

T he Natural History of Crickets

OF THE MANY INSECTS that are capable of producing sound in various ways, the best known and the most expert musicians are the crickets, who during the latter part of summer and in the autumn fill the air with a continuous concert. They are well known on account of their abundance, their wide distribution, their characteristic chirping song and the habit many of them have for seeking shelter in human habitations.

Crickets belong, in the entomological system, to the order Orthoptera (from the Greek *orthos*, "straight," and *pteron*, "a wing"; referring to the longitudinal folding of the hind wings). In this order the two pairs of wings differ in structure. The fore wings are parchment-like, forming covers for the more delicate hind wings. The wing-covers have received the special name *tegmina*; they are furnished with a fine network of veins, and overlap at the tip at least. There are many species in which the wings are rudimentary, even in the adult state. The order Orthoptera includes six families: the roaches, mantids, walkingsticks, locusts or short-horned grasshoppers, and the long-horned grasshoppers, including the katydids, and the crickets (*Gryllidae*). Of the crickets there are three distinct groups, known as mole crickets, true crickets, and tree crickets. ["True crickets" should read "field crickets". Mole crickets and tree crickets *are* true crickets.] The first named are so called because they burrow in the ground like moles; they are pre-eminently burrowers. The form of the body is suited to this mode of life. The front

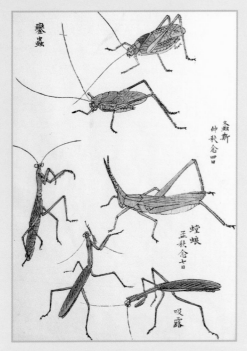

Wood-block print of insects. Height 10 ¼". Japan, 19th century.

tibiae, especially, are fitted for digging; they are greatly broadened, and shaped somewhat like hands or the feet of a mole. The mole-crickets feed upon the tender roots of various plants. The true crickets are common everywhere, living in fields, and some species even in our houses. They usually live on plants, but are not strictly vegetarians; sometimes they are predaceous and feed mercilessly upon other insects. The eggs are laid in the autumn, usually in the ground, and are hatched in the following summer. The greater number of the old insects die on the approach of winter; a few, however, survive the cold season. The tree crickets principally inhabit trees, but they occur also on shrubs, or even on high herbs and tall grass.

Like their near relatives, crickets have biting mouth parts, and, like the grasshoppers and katydids, rather long hind legs which render them fit for jumping. Although many of them have wings when full grown, they move about mainly by jumping or hopping. When the young cricket emerges from the egg, it strongly resembles the adult, but it lacks wings and wing-covers, which gradually appear as the insect grows older and larger. The final development of wings and wing-covers furnishes the means whereby the male cricket can produce his familiar chirping sound. It is only the adult male that sings; the young and the females cannot chirp.

The Science of Singing

ON EXAMINING THE BASE of the fore wings or wing-covers of the male cricket, it will be noticed that the veins at the base are fewer, thicker, and more irregular than those on the hind or lower wings. On the under side of some of these thick veins will also be seen fine, transverse ridges like those on a file. The wing-covers of the female have uniform, parallel veins, without a trace of ridges. The male cricket produces his chirping sound by raising his wing-covers above his body and then rubbing their bases together, so that the file-like veins of the under surface of the one wing-cover scrape the upper surface of the lower.

Only the wings of the male cricket have sound-producing attachments, and the males have them only when their wings are fully developed at the age of maturity. The young cricket has no wings.

Since crickets produce a characteristic sound, it is natural to suppose that both males and females are able to hear it. On the lower part of the fore legs of both sexes is found a little drum-like surface, which serves as the tympanum of an ear. The sound-producing organ and the ear of the katydids, which rank next to the crickets in their singing ability, are some-what similar in structure and location.

The sound made by crickets is, of course, not a true song, but a mechanical production, as are all of the sounds produced by insects. The object of the chirping or stridulating is somewhat conjectural. It may be a love-song, mating-call, or an expression of

Insects produce sound in two ways: by moving body parts against each other or by tapping on something. Oak bush crickets drum their feet on leaves to communicate with other crickets. The cicada makes sound by using tymbals on its abdomen.

Insects make sounds for different reasons: to attract the opposite sex, to locate their offspring, and to warn their insect neighbors of danger.

The cicada is one of the loudest insects. Its chirping can be heard from a quarter of a mile away. Not all insects make sound. Cave crickets cannot chirp, because they do not have wings.

*Eremobia magna. Lithograph.
America, 19th century.*

CLINT SHAW

Most cricket species are "right winged": their right wing folds over their left. The sounds they produce with their wings are genetic and species-specific. The chirp of each species has a distinctive frequency and pitch all its own. The chirps are so specific that they can be precisely measured. Scientists have found that temperature affects the rate of chirping. When carefully calibrated the chirp rate of some species can be used to measure the temperature.

Adult crickets can chirp continuously. The Chinese call this *lianbang* (continuous chirping).

The Chinese believe that because young crickets have just developed their wings they chirp in quick, short spurts called *labang*.

some other emotion. The fact that the crickets are able to sing only when they are full-grown and capable of mating would seem to suggest that their chirping is a love-song.

This commonly held view, however, is contested by Frank E. Lutz in an article on "Insect Sounds" published in *Natural History* (1926, No. 2). Dr. Lutz starts from the opinion that not everything in nature has a practical or utilitarian purpose and that many striking characters and characteristics of animals and plants are of no use to their possessors or to any other creature; they seem to him to be much like the figures in a kaleidoscope, definite and doubtless due to some internal mechanism, but not serving any special purpose. This highly trained entomologist then proceeds to observe, "The most familiar example of insect sounds made by friction is the chirping of crickets. Now, only the males do this. Chirping is distinctly a secondary sexual character, the stock explanation of which is that it is a mating-call developed by sexual selection. The adult life of a male cricket lasts a month or so, and he chirps most of the time, but he spends little of that time in mating. Why does he chirp when there is no female around? Possibly hoping that one will come; I do not know. When he has mated, his sexual life is done, but he keeps on chirping to his dying day. I do not know why; possibly to pass the time. I do not know this, however, and my knowledge is based on the breeding of literally thousands of crickets, while I was using them in a study of heredity: a female cricket pays but little attention to a chirping male. She may wave her antennae in his direction, but so will she when he is not chirping, and so will she at a stick or a stone." And the general conclusion Lutz arrives at is, "The significance of insect sounds is still an open subject and, while it is altogether probable that some of these sounds do have a biological significance, I firmly believe that many of them have none, being merely incidental to actions that are not intended to make a noise and to structures that have arisen for some totally different purpose or for no purpose at all." [Recent studies have shown that chirping (signaling behavior) is directly related to mating.]

The Chinese, perhaps, have made a not uninteresting contribution to this problem. Of the many species of crickets used by them, the females are kept only of one, – the black-tree cricket (*Homoeogryllus japonicus*), called by them *kin chung* [*jin zhong*] ("Golden Bell," with reference to its sounds), as they assert that this is the only kind of cricket that requires the presence of the female to sing. The females of all the other species are not kept by the Chinese. As soon as the insects are old enough that their sex can be determined, the females are fed to birds or sold to bird-fanciers. Accordingly, the males of all species kept in captivity by the Chinese, with a single exception, sing without the presence of the female. But whether captive insects are instructive examples for the study of the origin and motives of their chirps is another question. Our canaries and other birds in confinement likewise sing without females. Whatever the biological origin of insect sounds may be (and it is not necessary to assume that the sounds of all species must have sprung from the same causes), it seems reasonable to infer that the endless repetition of such sounds has the tendency to develop into a purely mechanical practice in which the insect indulges as a pastime for its own diversion. It is conceivable that insect music has little or nothing to do with the sex impulse, but that it is rather prompted by the instinct to play which is immanent in all animals.

Ceramic bird feeder with pair of crickets. 1½"h x 1"w. China, 20th century.

L' IMAGE ODIER-DANEE HAZAMA

Wood songbox with ivory accents for keeping singing insects. 2"w x 3"h. China, 20th century.

L' IMAGE ODIER-DANEE HAZAMA

Ivory insect cage. 2"h x 5"w. China, 19ᵗʰ century.

L' IMAGE ODIER-DANEE HAZAMA

Bugs in History

CLINT SHAW

Archaeological evidence points to a close relationship between the ancient people of China and their insect neighbors.

⚥ ⚥

The Dong Ba culture believed that silk worms, flies, bees and other insects played a key role in the creation of the world.

⚥ ⚥

The cicada motif appears on deer antlers unearthed at An-Yang (1766 BC) and bone spatulas from the Chou dynasty (1027 BC). Cricket-keeping containers have been found in Song dynasty (960 AD) tombs in Zhenjiang, China.

⚥ ⚥

Cicadas were buried with the dead as a symbol of resurrection during the Han dynasty (206 AD).

⚥ ⚥

The Chinese have been using gourds as insect cages and water vessels for centuries. In Yuyao county, archaeologists uncovered petrified gourd seeds that may be 7,000 years old.

⚥ ⚥

Today cicada molts are used in China to reduce fever, control skin eruptions and stop convulsions.

⚥ ⚥

According to the **BEN CAO GANG MU** (*Encyclopedia of Chinese Medicine*) by Li Shi-zheng (1578), dried katydids are aphrodisiacs. Because of this unique property, they were given to new parents as a symbol of fertility.

⚥ ⚥

Impressed gourd insect cage with the Eight Immortals design. Top is wood with ivory goldfish. 4"h. China, 20th century.

Nomenclature

THE RELATION OF THE CHINESE TO THE CRICKETS and other insects presents one of their most striking characteristics and one of the most curious chapters of culture-historical development. In the primitive stages of life [the Neolithic period] man took a keen interest in the animal world, and first of all, he closely observed and studied large mammals, and next to these, birds and fishes. A curious exception to this almost universal rule is presented by the ancient Chinese. In accordance with their training and the peculiar direction in which their imaginative and observational powers were led, they were more interested in the class of insects than in all other groups of animals combined; while mammals, least of all, attracted their attention. [Insects did play an important role in China's cultural development, but were not, as Laufer suggests, of primary focus in comparison to other animals.] Their love of insects led them to observations and discoveries which still elicit our admiration. The curious life-history of the cicada was known to them in early times, and only a nation which had an innate sympathy with the smallest creatures of nature was able to penetrate into the mysterious habits of the silkworm and present the world with the discovery of silk. The cicada as an emblem of resurrection, the praying mantis as a symbol of bravery, and many other insects play a prominent role in early religious and poetical conceptions as well as in art, as shown by their effigies in jade.

The **ER-YA** (500-200 BC) was the first scientific work in China to organize and name living things. Insects are among the entries.

❈

In addition to their scientific names, insects often have colloquial names, like *jiao ge-ge* (singing brother) and *jie-er* (singing sister). In Southern China, the *ban'ger tou* insect is also called *guan cai tou* (coffin head) because of the shape of its head.

❈

Wood-block print of insects. Japan.

CLINT SHAW

In regard to mammals, birds, and fishes, Chinese terminology does not rise above the ordinary, but their nomenclature of insects is richer and more colorful than that of most languages. Not only do they have a distinct word or even several terms for every species found in their country, but also numerous poetic and local names for the many varieties of each species for which words are lacking in English and other tongues.

Moulded gourd insect cage. Ivory lid has lotus flowers. 3¹/₂"h. China, 20ᵗʰ century.

ricket Books

CORRESPONDING TO THEIR FONDNESS FOR CRICKETS, the Chinese have developed a special literature on the subject. The first of these works is the *Tsu chi king* ("Book of Crickets") written by Kia Se-tao, a minister of state, who lived in the first part of the thirteenth century, under the Sung dynasty. His book, continued and provided with additional matter by Chou Li-tsing of the Ming period, is still in existence, and has remained the most important and authoritative treatise on the subject, which has been freely drawn upon by all subsequent writers. The author, a passionate cricket fancier himself, gives minute descriptions and subtle classifications of all species and varieties of crickets known to him and dwells at length on their treatment and care. Under the title *Tsu chi chi* ("Records of Crickets") a similar booklet was produced by Liu Tung under the Ming dynasty. During the Manchu period, Fang Hu wrote a *Tsu chi p'u* ("Treatise on Crickets"), and Ch'en Hao-tse, in his *Hua king* ("Mirror of Flowers") written in 1688, offers several interesting sections on crickets.

Impressed gourd insect cage with Chinese character meaning "long life." Wood top with ivory birds and flowers. 4½"h. China, 20ᵗʰ century.

L' IMAGE ODIER-DANEE HAZAMA

PICTURED LEFT:
Gourd insect cage. Impressed landscape scene with animals. Wood top has ivory dragon and phoenix. 4½"h. China, 20ᵗʰ century.

L' IMAGE ODIER-DANEE HAZAMA

Molded gourd insect cages for katydids and zhazui are fitted with a huang (metal coil) that prevents the insect from jumping out and protects its antennae. Ivory kou (lip) and gourd top (piaogai). 4" h. China, 20th century.

L' IMAGE ODIER-DANEE HAZAMA

The Rise of the Cricket Cult

IN THEIR RELATIONS TO CRICKETS the Chinese have passed through three distinct periods: during the first period running, from the times of early antiquity down to the T'ang dynasty, they merely appreciated the cricket's powerful tunes; under the Táng (A.D. 618-906) they began to keep crickets as interned prisoners in cages to be able to enjoy their concert at any time; finally, under the Sung (A.D. 960-1278) they developed the sport of cricket fights and a regular cult of the cricket.

Moulded gourd insect cage. Wood top has inset polished walnut shell. 5" h. China, 20th century.

Impressed gourd insect cage with characters. Wood top has inset ivory fish. 4 ½"h. China, 20th century.

Insect keeping was once considered a distinguished hobby. Chinese painters, poets, musicians and officials all kept pet insects. There were societies for all levels of hobbyists. The emperor even had eunuchs to tend to his beloved singing pets.

After 1949, cricket breeding and gourd molding declined. Critics claimed it was a petty diversion. By the 1960s, most of the gourd artists and insect keepers were gone.

The life cycles of insects play an important role in agrarian societies like China. When the insects begin to hatch, farmers know that spring is coming. The Chinese solar calendar designates a day in February as *Jing-Zhe* (Waking of the Insects).

Songbox for keeping insects. Wood with ivory accents. 2"h x 3"w. China, 20th century.

Cricket Songs

THE PRAISE OF THE CRICKET is sung in the odes of the *Shi king*, the earliest collection of Chinese popular songs. People then enjoyed listening to its chirping sounds, while it moved about in their houses and under their beds. It was regarded as a creature of good omen, and wealth was predicted for the families which had many crickets on their hearths. When their voices were heard in the autumn, it was a signal for the weavers to commence their work.

The sounds produced by the mitred cricket (*Gryllus mitratus*: Plate 2, Fig. 2, page 19) recall to the Chinese the click of a weaver's shuttle. One of its names therefore is *tsu-chi*, which means literally "one who stimulates spinning." "Chicken of the weaver's shuttle" is a term of endearment for it.

One of the songs in the *Shi king* consists of three stanzas each of which begins, "The cricket is in the hall." The time intended is the ninth month when the year entered on its last quarter. In another song of the same collection it is said, "The *se chung* [a kind of cricket] moves its legs; in the sixth month, the spinner [another species of cricket] sounds its wings; in the seventh month it is in the wilderness; in the eighth month it is under the eaves; in the ninth month it is around the doors; in the tenth month the cricket enters under our beds."

At this point the Chinese are not distinguished from other nations. Our word "cricket" is imitative of the sound of the insect (literally, "little creaker," derived from French *criquer*, "to creak").

14

Literary Bugs

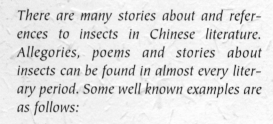

IN OLD ENGLAND it was considered a sign of good fortune to have a cricket chirping by the hearth, and to kill one of these harmless little creatures was looked upon as a breach of hospitality. Their cheerful tunes suggested peace and comfort, the coziness of the homely fireside. They were harbingers of good luck and joy. Gower, in his *Pericles*, offers the verse:

> *And crickets sing at the oven's mouth,*
> *E'er the blither for their drouth.*

Ben Jonson (*Bartholomew Fair*) alludes to the insect's tunes thus: "Walk as if thou hadst borrowed legs of a spinner and voice of a cricket." Shakespeare has several references to this lover of the fireside whose note is so suggestive of cozy comfort. Milton (*Il Penseroso*, 81) has the line:

> *Far from all resort of mirth*
> *Save the cricket on the hearth.*

On the other hand, the tunes of the hidden melodist were regarded by many persons with superstition and awe, and were believed to be an omen of sorrow and evil; its voice even predicted the death of a member of the family (see J. Brand, *Observations on the Popular Antiquities of Great Britain*, 1888, Vol 3, p.189).

There are many stories about and references to insects in Chinese literature. Allegories, poems and stories about insects can be found in almost every literary period. Some well known examples are as follows:

A BRIEF ACCOUNT OF THE SIGHTS AND THINGS OF THE IMPERIAL COURT
by Liu Tong

NOTES ON NEW YEAR BUSTLING IN THE IMPERIAL CAPITAL
by Pan Rongbi

NOTES ON BEIJING'S FESTIVITIES
by Fucha Dun Chong

A CLASSIFIED COLLECTION OF QING LITERATURE
by Xu Ke

Western literature, when compared to the literature of China, has relatively few mentions of insects.   A few Western writers have mentioned insects in their work:

Jonathan Swift in **GULLIVER'S TRAVELS**

Edgar Allen Poe in **THE GOLD BUG**

Henry David Thoreau in **WALDEN**

Lewis Carroll in **THROUGH THE LOOKING GLASS**

Vladimir Nabokov in **SPEAK, MEMORY**

Franz Kafka, **METAMORPHOSIS**

PICTURED RIGHT:
Ink painting of cicada. Anonymous. China, 20th century.

CLINT SHAW

No one, however, has depicted the cricket's chirping with more poetic insight and charm than Charles Dickens in his immortal story *The Cricket on the Hearth*, in describing the competition between the cricket and the boiling kettle.

And here, if you like, the Cricket did chime in! with a Chirrup, Chirrup, Chirrup of such magnitude, by way of chorus; with a voice, so astoundingly disproportionate to its size, as compared with the Kettle; (size! you couldn't see it!) that if it had then and there a burst itself like an overcharged gun, if it had fallen victim on the spot, and chirruped its little body into fifty pieces, it would have seemed a natural and inevitable consequence, for which it had expressly laboured.

The Kettle had had the last of its solo performance. It persevered with undiminished ardour; but the Cricket took first fiddle and kept it. Good Heaven, how it chirped! Its shrill, sharp, piercing voice resounded through the house, and seemed to twinkle in the outer darkness like a Star. There was an indescribable little trill and tremble in it, at its loudest, which suggested its being carried off its legs, and made to leap again, by its own intense enthusiasm. Yet they went very well together, the Cricket and the Kettle. The burden of the song was still the same; and louder, louder, louder still, they sang it in their emulation.

The cricket now began to chirp again, vehemently.

'Heyday!' said John, in his slow way. 'It's merrier than ever, to-night, I think.'

'And it's sure to bring us good fortune, John! It always has done so. To have a Cricket on the Hearth, is the luckiest thing in all the world!'

John looked at her as if he had very nearly got the thought into his head, that she was his Cricket in chief, and he quite agreed with her. But it was probably one of his narrow escapes, for he said nothing.

'The first time I heard its cheerful little note, John, was on that night when you brought me home- when you brought me to my new home here; its little mistress. Nearly a year ago. You recollect, John?'

'Oh yes,' John remembered. 'I should think so!'

'Its chirp was such a welcome to me! It seemed so full of promise and encouragement. It seemed to say, you would be kind and gentle with me, and would not expect (I had a fear of that, John, then) to find an old head on the shoulders of your foolish little wife.'

....'It spoke the truth, John, when it seemed to say so; for you have ever been, I am sure, the best, the most considerate, the most affectionate of husbands to me. This has been a happy home, John; and I love the Cricket for its sake!'....

'I love it for the many times I have heard it, and the many thoughts its harmless music has given me'.

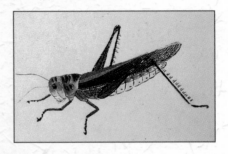

Ink painting of grasshopper. Anonymous. China, 20th century.

CLINT SHAW

PLATE I

BOYS PLAYING WITH CRICKETS
Scene from Chinese painting of the twelfth century in the Field Museum of Natural History, Chicago.

*I*nsects Kept as Pets

THE CHINESE BOOK *T'IEN PAO I SHI* ("*Affairs of the Period T'ien-pao,*" A.D. 742-756) contains the following notice:–

Whenever the autumnal season arrives, the ladies of the palace catch crickets in small golden cages. These with the cricket enclosed in them they place near their pillows, and during the night hearken to the voices of the insects. This custom was imitated by all people.

As it happened in China so frequently, a certain custom first originated in the palace, became fashionable, and then gradually spread among all classes of the populace. The women enshrined in the imperial seraglio evidently found solace and diversion in the company of crickets during their lonesome nights. Instead of golden cages, the people availed themselves of small bamboo or wooden cages which they carried in their bosom or suspended from their girdles.

The museum [the Field Museum of Natural History in Chicago] owns a valuable painting in the form of a long roll depicting the games and pastimes of a hundred boys and attributed to Su Han-ch'en, a renowned artists of the twelfth century: one of the scenes shows six boys surrounded by crickets jars, one of them holding a tickler and letting a cricket out of a trap-box into a jar (Plate 1).

In Plates 2 and 3 the principal species of crickets kept by the Chinese in Peking are illustrated from actual specimens obtained. . . . Most of the genera belong to the family *Gryllidae*, only two to the family *Tettigoniidae*: *Gampsocleis inflata* Uvarov and *G. gratiosa*, subspecies *infuscata* Uvarov, the latter illustrated in Plate 3, Fig. 3. The besprinkled cricket (*Gryllus conspersus* Schaum, Chinese *si-so*), figured in Plate 2, Fig.1, is common all over China, and is also known from the Luchu Islands, Hawaii, and the East Indies. The mitred cricket (*Gryllus mitratus* Burmeister) in Plate 2, Fig. 2, is known from most countries of Eastern Asia, particularly China, Korea, Japan, Tonking, and the Malay Archipelago. The broad-faced cricket (*Loxoblemmus taicoun* Saussure) in Plate 2, Fig. 3, has also been described from Japan and Java.

The yellowish tree-cricket (*Oecanthus rufescens* Serville: Plate 3, Fig.1) is a favorite with the people of both Peking and Shanghai; it occurs also in the East Indies, but is quite distinct from *O. longicauda Matsumura* of Japan. The black tree-cricket (*Homoeogryllus japonicus* Haan: Plate 3, Fig. 2), the "Golden Bell" (*kin chung*) [*jin zhong*] of the Chinese because its sound is compared with that of a bell, is very popular in Peking; it is also known from Japan, Java, and northern India. It is evident that the large, glossy black insect in Plate 3, Fig.3, is quite different from the crickets and, as mentioned, is placed by us in a separate family. The Chinese also distinguish it from the cricket and bestow on it the peculiar name *yu-hu-lu* which is imitative of its sound; this word belongs to the colloquial language, there is no literary name for this insect.

As to color, green, black, yellow, and purple crickets are distinguished by the Chinese, the green and black ones taking the first rank.

The notes of the Golden Bell are described as being like the tinkling of a small bell, and its stridulation is characterized with the words *teng ling ling*. The

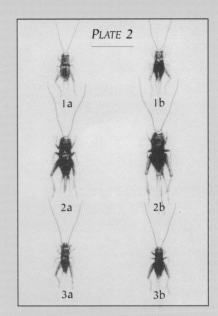

CRICKETS OF CHINA (a. male; b. female)
1. Besprinkled Cricket, *Gryllus conspersus* Schaum. 2. Mitrid Cricket, *Gryllus mitratus* Burmeister. Chinese *se-so* or *ts'u-chi*, Peking colloquial *ch'ü*. 3. Broad-faced Cricket, *Loxoblemmus taicoun* Saussure. Chinese *pang-t'ou* (Watchman's Rattle)

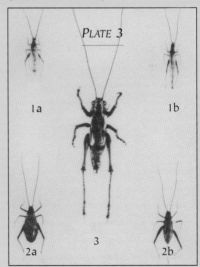

CRICKETS OF CHINA (a. male; b. female)
1. Yellowish Tree Cricket, *Oecanthus rufescens* Serville. Chinese *kwo-lou*, Peking colloquial *kwo-kwo*. 2. Black Tree Cricket, *Homoeogryllus japonicus* Haan. Chinese *kin chung* (Golden Bell). 3. Infuscated Shield-backed Katydid, *Gampsocleis gratiosa infuscata* Uvarov. Peking-Chinese *yu-hu-lu*.

Moulded gourd insect cage.
Wood top has carved dragon.
China, 20ᵗʰ century.

L' IMAGE ODIER-DANEE HAZAMA

Jin zhong (golden bells) should be kept in pairs so they require a cage with a large base, like the one shown here.

Gourds can be shaped by a variety of methods. A fabric band was tied around this gourd to narrow its waist as it grew.

Japanese designate this species "bell-insect" (*suzu-mushi*). Lafcadio Hearn, who in his essay "Insect-Musicians" describes the various kinds of crickets favored by the Japanese, says that the bell of which the sound is thus referred to is a very small bell, or a bunch of little bells, such as a Shinto priestess uses in the sacred dances. He writes, further, that this species is a great favorite with insect-fanciers in Japan, and is bred in great numbers for the market. In the wild state it is found in many parts of Japan. The Japanese compare it with a watermelon seed, as it is very small, has a black back, and a white or yellowish belly. This insect, according to the Chinese, stridulates only at night and stops at dawn; the concert produced by a chorus causes a deafening din which is characterized by Hearn as a sound like rapids, and by a Chinese author as the sound of drums and trumpets.

Chinese authors know correctly that the "voices" of crickets, as they say, are produced by the motion of their wings. The stridulatory sounds are described by them as *tsa-tsa* or *sat-tsat*, also as *tsi-tsi*. The term *kwo-kwo* for the yellowish tree-cricket (Plate 3, Fig. 1) also is onomatopoetic. Terms of endearment for a cricket are "horse of the hearth," "chick of the hearth," "chick of the god of the hearth."

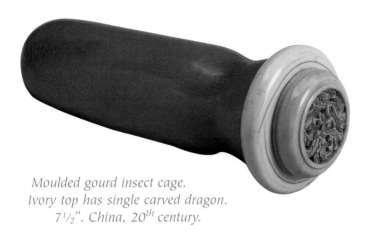

Moulded gourd insect cage.
Ivory top has single carved dragon.
7¹/₂". China, 20ᵗʰ century.

The shape of the gourd, like the shape of a musical instrument, is important because it determines the tone of the insect's chirp. The lid is equally important. Its thickness and the number and diameter of holes effect the sound of the insect.

Moulded gourd insect cage with
applied four seasons pattern.
Ivory top with iris. 3¹/₂". China, 20ᵗʰ century.

Perhaps the most popular insects kept as pets in China are *guoguo, zhazui, youhulu, qugu, bang'er tou* and *jin zhong.*

⋆ ⋆

Katydids (*guoguo*) are popular, because they breed late in the autumn and last through the winter. *Guoguo* with long, wide legs are the best singers.

⋆ ⋆

Zhazui are similar to katydids but smaller. In South China they are called *zha'er.* These insects are imported to Beijing from Shandong Province.

⋆ ⋆

Youhulu are large crickets, popular for their pleasant chirping song.

⋆ ⋆

Qugu are a small variety of cricket.

⋆ ⋆

Bang'ertou should be kept in long-necked gourd cages to prevent them from jumping out.

⋆ ⋆

Jin zhong (golden bells) are available at the street market in Beijing in August. Insect vendors say they are caught in the Ming tombs of Yizhou.

⋆ ⋆

PICTURED RIGHT: Some insect vendors, like this one in North China, journey far into the countryside in search of prize insects to sell at the market. Each woven bamboo basket contains an insect.

Insect keepers wax the wings of their favorite singers to amplify their chirping. The waxing process, called *dian yiao* or *zhan yiao*, is a delicate procedure. A bit of cypress or lacebark pine sap is mixed with cinnabar to make a bright red wax. After heating, it is applied to the wings of the insect. Only a tiny drop of wax, heated to the perfect temperature, is applied. If the wax is too hot or if too much is applied, it can injure or kill the insect. A small amount of wax is applied both to the top wing (*gaiyao*) and the bottom wing (*diyao*). The application and placement of the wax varies, depending on the size and type of insect.

Insects with unwaxed wings (*benjiao*) are kept in small cages, because their chirping sound cannot be heard from within a large cage.

L' IMAGE ODIER-DANEE HAZAMA

Catching Crickets

THERE ARE VARIOUS METHODS of catching crickets. They are usually captured at evening. In the north of China a lighted candle is placed near the entrance of their hole, and a trap box is held in readiness. Attracted by the light, the insects hop out of their retreats, and are finally caught in the traps made of bamboo or ivory rods. Some of these ivory traps are veritable works of art: they are surmounted by carvings of dragons, and the trap doors shut very accurately (Plate 10, Figs. 1 and 2, page 34). The doors are shown open in the illustration.

The trap shown in Fig. 4 of the same Plate is an oblong, rectangular wooden box, as used in central China; the trap door at the end of the box is a plain wooden slip fitting into a groove, which may be lifted and lowered in a few seconds.

In the south, men avail themselves of what is called a fire-basket (*fo lam*) which is made of iron rods and in which a charcoal fire is kept burning. This fire drives the insects out of their dens. Sometimes the cricket-hunters reach their object by pouring water into the holes where the insects hide. Sometimes they endeavor to entice them from the nest by placing at its entrance the fruit of *Nephelium longana* (*lung yen*, "dragon's eyes").

In Shanghai and Hangchow grasshoppers are also held captives and enclosed in wooden cages, usually of the shape of a chair, stool, or table (Plate 5).

PLATE 4 AND PLATE 5

CAGES FOR GRASSHOPPERS IN SHAPE OF WOODEN CHAIR AND TABLE. Enclosed by glass. Hangchow, China.

Most pet insects are bought at the markets from the breeders, except for the katydids which are caught in the wild.

❧ ❧

Catching katydids is no easy task. They are well camouflaged and quick jumpers. The best way to catch them is with a wire basket and a pair of gloves.

❧ ❧

Like the katydids, golden bells (*jin zhong*) are difficult to catch. One popular method is to leave a hollowed-out, inverted melon rind on the ground. During the night, the insects hide underneath where they can be captured in the morning.

❧ ❧

Earlier this century, the most famous places to hunt for katydids around Beijing were the Huiyu and Mengwo valleys.

❧ ❧

Cicadas were formerly also kept in small cages which were suspended at the eaves of houses or from the branches of trees, but this custom is no longer practised. The cicada is at present not offered for sale in the markets like the cricket. It may occasionally be caught by boys and caged by them for their amusement temporarily, but otherwise interest in this insect has waned. The same holds good for Japan, where cicadas are never caged. Japanese poets, as Lafcadio Hearn observes, are much more inclined to praise the voices of night-crickets than those of cicadas; there are countless poems about the latter, but very few which commend their singing.

Bamboo insect trapping cage with sliding door.
3½"w x 4"h. China, 20ᵗʰ century.

L' IMAGE ODIER-DANEE HAZAMA

Man examining a cricket at the street market in Beijing, China.

The best singing insects have thick wings with wide veins. Their wings should be close together and fit snugly against their bodies. Loose (*hefeng*) or sagging wings (*palabang*) do not produce a pleasing tone.

When purchased from the street market or carried around town, the insect's cage should be kept in a *tao* (a drawstring silk bag) to protect the cage from damage and to keep the insect warm.

Different types of insects prefer different temperatures. Crickets like to be kept in a jacket pocket where it is warm, but not too hot. Katydids like warmer temperatures. They prefer to be kept closer to the body. Inside a shirt pocket is the best place.

TOP: *Beijing, China.* CHINASTOCK
BELOW: *This insect cage is curved to fit comfortably against the body.*

L' IMAGE ODIER-DANEE HAZAMA

Cricket Raising

MANY PEOPLE REAR HUNDREDS OF CRICKETS in their homes, and have several rooms stacked with jars which shelter the insects. The rich employ experts to look after theirs. As soon as you enter a house like this, you are greeted by a deafening noise which a Chinese is able to stand for any length of time.

During the summer the insects are kept in circular pottery jars made of a common burnt clay and covered with a flat lid, which is sometimes perforated. Many potters made a special business of these cricket houses, and impressed on them a seal with their names; for instance, Chao Tse-yu, who lived in the first part of the nineteenth century and whose productions still enjoy a special reputation. There are old pots said to go back as far as the Ming dynasty (1368-1643), and these are highly prized. The crickets keep cool in these jars, which are often shaped in the form of a gourd, as the heat does not penetrate the thick clay walls. Tiny porcelain dishes decorated in blue and white or small bits of clay contain food and water for the insects, and they are also provided with beds or sleeping boxes of clay (Plates 6 and 11, pages 28 and 39). Jars of somewhat larger size serve for holding the cricket-fights.

The jars were decorated with the auspicious symbols of bats, phoenix birds, dragons and lotus flowers. The best quality jars were made from *chen ni* clay, a special clay that is tied in a silk bag and soaked in water for many years before it is used.

Miniature dishes and ivory cage.

L' IMAGE ODIER–DANEE HAZAMA

Raising insects (*fen*) is a delicate matter. Insect breeders, like Zhao Zichen and Wang Zhen of Beijing, mastered the process and were sought after by insect fanciers who bought choice insects from them each season.

The katydids are raised in baskets with soil in the bottom. After the eggs are laid the soil is sifted and the eggs are caught in a sieve. Then they are transferred to a pot of sand, placed in a sunny window and misted daily.

When the eggs hatch, they are fed masticated beans and sheep liver.

After the fifth shed, the insects are given a sorghum stalk to climb on. They will hang upside down and molt. This is a trying time for insects and breeders alike. Many breeders stay awake all night to make sure the molt is successful.

After reaching maturity, insects are transferred from their jars to gourd cages, so that they may be carried around.

Ground dwelling insect's cages are filled with a special mixture called *diandi* (base fill). *Diandi*, a mixture of clay, lime and fine sand is sifted and mixed with water before being poured into the bottom of the gourd. The placement of the *diandi* is very important, because it influences the acoustics of the gourd. The *diandi* should always be placed at a twenty to thirty degree slant with the upper edge of the soil just reaching the waist of the gourd. The mixture is then smoothed with a tool called a *yazi*. After smoothing, the soil is hard and shiny. When dry, it is glazed with Chinese herbs called *hai' ercha* (children's tea).

Clay sleeping box for use in a cricket jar. 2½"w x ½"h. China, 20th century.

L' IMAGE ODIER-DANEE HAZAMA

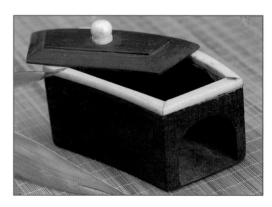

Wood sleeping box with a removable lid and ivory trim. China, 20th century.

L' IMAGE ODIER-DANEE HAZAMA

Some modern cricket breeders use layers of egg cartons to provide hiding places for their crickets. An inverted water bottle and a damp sponge provide water.
BELOW: Adult Crickets.

PHOTOS ON THIS PAGE BY CLINT SHAW

FROM BOTTOM RIGHT TO TOP LEFT:
1/8" baby cricket
1/4" two week old cricket
1/2" three week old cricket
3/4" four week old cricket
1" juvenile/adult cricket

In Beijing, cricket breeders are called *guanjia* (jar men).

Breeders keep up to thirty crickets in a one gallon *ziguan* (egg jar). Breeding colonies have an equal number of male and female crickets.

Hiding places are provided to keep the crickets from injuring themselves or eating each other. Two inches of soil in the bottom insulates the *ziguan* and provides substrate for laying eggs. The *ziguan* is kept on a *kuang* (heated bed) to keep the temperature around eighty degrees Fahrenheit.

Crickets will drown in a bowl of water, so a piece of damp cloth or sponge is added as a water source. They are fed a diet of vegetables and 20 percent protein.

Females can be easily distinguished from males, because they have ovipositors, for egg laying that protrude from their hind quarters.

Eggs are laid in the soil substrate and take about two weeks to hatch. Each egg is about $1/16$" long and looks like white rice. The optimal life span of a cricket is eight to twelve weeks.

Some breeders suppress the hatching of the eggs by adjusting the heat and humidity. The insects hatch later, enabling them to last through the winter. This process called *yazi* (suppressing the eggs) is known only to the best insect breeders.

One of Beijing's best-known cage makers was Shao Bai. His cages were unique because they incorporated blemishes from nature in the decorative designs. A gourd with marks left by nibbling birds or insects called *yingshang* (tough wounds), with water-spots called *yin pi* (shaded skin), or with leaf marks called *yeda* all became works of art in his hands.

Gourds make ideal cricket cages because they are easy to grow, lightweight, portable, heat retaining, and their soft texture enhances the song of the cricket.

Cricket Cages

DURING THE WINTER MONTHS the crickets change their home, and are transferred to specially prepared gourds which are provided with loose covers wrought in open work so as to admit fresh air into the gourd. This is said to be a special variety of the common gourd (*Lagenaria vulgaris*), the cultivation of which was known to a single family of Peking. . . . The gourds used as cricket habitations are all artificially shaped; they are raised in earthen moulds, the flowers are forced into the moulds, and as they grow will assume the shape of and the designs fashioned in the moulds. There is accordingly an infinite variety of forms: there are slender and graceful, round and double, cylindrical and jar-like ones. . . . The technique employed in these ancient pieces is now lost; at least they are no longer made, though there are poor modern imitations in which the surfaces are carved, not moulded.

The covers of the gourd, flat or tall, are made of jade, elephant or walrus ivory, coconut shell, and sandalwood, all elaborately decorated, partly in high relief, partly in open work, or in the two methods combined, with floral designs, dragons, lions and other animals. Gourd vines with flowers and fruits belong to the most favorite designs carved in the flat ivory covers; gourd and cricket appear to be inseparable companions. A kind of cement which is a mixture of lime and sandy loam is smeared over the bottom of the gourd to provide a comfortable resting-place for the tenant. The owner of the cricket may carry the gourd in his bosom wherever he goes, and in passing men in the street you may hear the shrill sound of the insect from its warm and safe place of refuge. The gourds keep the insects warm, and on a cold night they receive a cotton padding to sleep upon.

Plain gourds are illustrated in Plates 7 and 8, Figs. 1-2; decorated ones, in Plates 8, Figs.3-4, and 9.

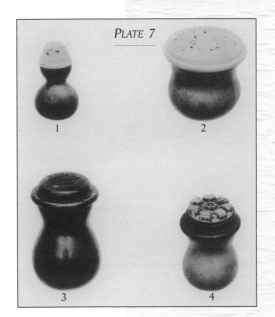

CRICKET GOURDS. The winter habitations of the insects. 1-2. Covers of ivory carved in open work. 3. Cover of carved coconut-shell. 4. Cover of sandalwood decorated with eight auspicious Buddhistic emblems.

CRICKET GOURDS. 1. Cover of ivory. 2. Cover of white jade. 3. With moulded designs of dragons. 4. Coated with red lacquer in two layers. Cover of ivory with carving of three lions playing ball.

CRICKET GOURDS. With moulded decorations; scenery, figures, and ornaments. The figure in the centre represents a carved walnut shell an enlargement of which is shown in Plate 12.

Connoisseurs divide gourd cages into two categories: those that were officially molded in the palaces of high officials called *guan muzi* (official mold) and those that were made by commoners.

❋

Gourds with pointed bottoms are called spider-bellied gourds. Gourds with turns smaller than their bellies are called *kuifan*. Gourds with turns larger than their bellies are called *chafan*. Long necked gourds are called *yanbo* (gander neck) and gourds that are round and shiny are called "monk head" gourds. Gourds that have a natural shape and have not been molded are called *benzhang*.

❋

The best cages have thick rinds and are well proportioned. Good quality antique cages often have a glossy patina from years of being caressed by their owners. Some present-day dealers have been known to stain and oil contemporary cages to give them the well-used antique look.

❋

Gourd cages made by skilled artisans are avidly collected by insect fanciers. One of Beijing's most famous cricket keepers and collectors was Sun Hou (Sun the Monkey). He had a reputation for being a ruthless bargainer and zealous collector.

❋

Artisans employed a number of techniques including engraving, etching, molding, and carving to create a large variety of cages.

Mengxin - Different types of lids have different names. Flat lids, like this one, are called *piaoxin*. Bulging lids are called *mantouding* (steam bun). Lids with moving parts are called *dongxinzi* or *dongmengxin*. Tall *mengxin* of ivory, jade, tortoise shell, wood, horn and other precious materials are beautiful, but they topple over easily and adversely affect the insect's chirping tone.

蒙心

Kuang (or Kuangzi) - Like the *mengxin*, the *kuang* is made from precious materials. Its thickness varies, depending on the type of *mengxin* and the desired proportions of the cage.

框

Kou - The *kou* is made from a variety of materials including wood, ivory and horn. Before 1930, thin *kou* were fashionable. This cage has a very thick *kou*.

口

Fan - The best gourds are called *santin yucheng* (three parts in even proportion), meaning that the *du, bo* and *fan* are aesthetically balanced.

翻

Bo - The *bo* of the gourd varies, depending on the type of insect kept inside.

脖

Yao - The *yao* is measured by the number of fingers that can fit in the opening. This measurement is used to determine which type of insect is best for a cage. Katydids require the most space, about four fingers of space. The cricket needs the least, about one and a half fingers of space.

腰

Du - If the insect is a ground dweller, this area is filled with soil. Otherwise, it is left empty.

肚

Pingtuo or dituo - A *pingtuo* is added as a base to keep the gourd sitting upright.

平托或底托

DIAGRAM ADAPTED FROM WANG, 1993

_F_ood Fit for the Emperor

IN THE SUMMER the insects are generally fed on fresh cucumber, lettuce, and other greens. During their confinement in autumn and winter masticated chestnuts and yellow beans are given them. In the south they are also fed on chopped fish and various kinds of insects, and even receive honey as a tonic. It is quite a common sight to see the idlers congregated in the tea-houses and laying their crickets out on the tables. Their masters wash the gourds with hot tea and chew chestnuts and beans to feed them. Then they listen to their songs and boast of their grinding powers. The Chinese cricket books give many elaborate rules for proper feeding which vary with the different species and with every month. The Golden Bell, for instance, should be fed on wormwood (or southern-wood, _ts'ing hao, Artemisia apiacea_), while flowers of the "silk melon" (_Luffa cylindrica_) and melon pulp are prescribed for the Spinning Damsel.

The fighting crickets receive particular attention and nourishment, a dish consisting of a bit of rice mixed with fresh cucumbers, boiled chestnuts, lotus seeds, and mosquitoes. When the time for the fight draws near, they get a tonic in the form of a bouillon made from the root of a certain flower. Some fanciers allow themselves to be stung by mosquitoes, and when these are full of blood, they are given their favorite pupils. In order to stir their ferocity prior to a bout, they are sometimes also compelled to fast. As soon as they recognize from their slow movements that they are sick, they are fed on small red insects gathered in water.

Katydids are especially fond of melon, bean sprouts and radish. They also like an occasional live worm.

Cicadas live in trees and eat tree sap.

Jinz hong like green stalk vegetables.

Each year cricket fanciers from miles around met at a neighborhood teahouse for the annual "Chirping at the Lantern" festival (_Jiaodeng_) to show off their best singers.

Ceramic insect feeding dishes. ¾" to 1". China.

33

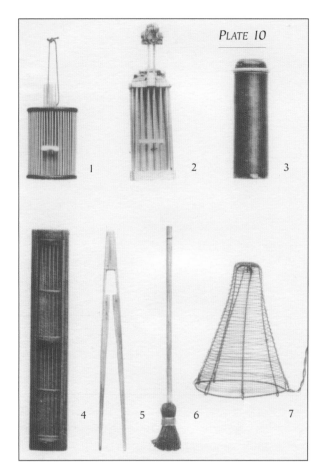

PLATE 10

Accessories.
1, 2, 4. Traps for catching insects, 1 and 4 of bamboo, 2 of ivory. 3. Gourd of cylindrical shape for keeping female crickets to secure eggs. 5. Pair of nippers for taking feeding-dishes out or in. 6. Brush for cleaning cricket-pots and gourds. 7. Wire frame under which crickets are held while their cages are being cleaned.

*I*nsect Concerts

A TICKLER IS USED FOR STIRRING the crickets to incite them to sing. In Peking fine hair from hare or rat whiskers inserted in a reed or bone handle is utilized for this purpose; in Shanghai, a fine blade of crab or finger grass (*Panicum syntherisma*). The ticklers are kept in bamboo or wooden tubes. . . . A special brush serves for cleaning the gourds and jars (Plate 10, Fig. 6); and a pair of wooden nippers or tongs is used for handling the food and water dishes (Plate 10, Fig.5). The insect is held under a wire screen, while its gourd is being cleaned or washed (Plate 10, Fig.7). A hair net enclosed in a hoop is placed over the jar to watch the doing of the insects (Plate 6, in the upper right corner).

The tympanum of good singers is coated with a bit of wax to increase or strengthen the volume of sound. A small needle about three inches long with blunt end, about the size of a darning needle, is heated over a candle and lightly dipped in the wax. The insect is held between the thumb and forefinger of the closed hand, and the wax is applied to the wing-covers. . . .

Cricket tickler storage container. China.

L' IMAGE ODIER-DANEE HAZAMA

One autumn day in the Qing dynasty while tending to the emperor's insects, a eunuch made an astonishing discovery. He noticed that the cricket in the cage he had hung in the pine tree for the emperor's enjoyment had an unusually beautiful voice. Upon closer examination, he discovered that some tree sap had dripped on to the cricket's wings, heightening the chirping sound. From that day forward, waxed-wing crickets became fashionable.

Cricket Fighting

CRICKETS ARE IMBUED with the natural instinct to fight. The Chinese offer the following explanation for this fact: the crickets live in holes, and each hole is inhabited by a single individual; this manner of living gives rise to frictions and frequent combats, for the insects always prefer their old places of refuge, and when they encounter in them another inmate, they will not cede their rights voluntarily, but will at once start to fight over the housing problem. The two rivals will jump at each other's heads with furious bites, and the combat will usually end in the death of one of the fighters. It frequently happens that the victor devours the body of his adversary, just as primitive man did away with the body of his enemy whom he had slain in mortal strife. When driven by hunger, crickets will feed upon other insects and even devour their own relations. When several are confined in a cage, they do not hesitate to eat one another. War and death is a law of nature.

In the course of many generations, the Chinese through long experience and practice, have accomplished what we may call a natural selection of fighting crickets. The good fighters are believed to be incarnations of great heroes of the past, and are treated in every respect like soldiers. Kia Se-tao, the first author who wrote on the subject, says that "rearing crickets is like rearing soldiers." The strongest and bravest of these who are most appreciated at Peking and Tientsin come from the southern province of Kwang-tung. These fighters are dubbed "generals" or "marshals," and seven varieties of them are distinguished, each with a special name.

The *qugu* (also called *xishuai* and *cu zhi*) are champion fighters. Broad backs and large heads are characteristics of winning crickets.

Three boys fighting crickets. Beijing, China.

During the early years of the Qing dynasty the Ministry of Textiles organized national cricket fighting matches every autumn. Gamblers bet large sums of money on favorite crickets. Fortunes were lost and families were destroyed. As a result, cricket fighting was officially prohibited by the end of the Qing dynasty.

Clay figurine of two men fighting crickets.
4"h. China, 20th century.

L' IMAGE ODIER–DANEE HAZAMA

Those with black heads and gray hair in their bodies are considered best. Next in appreciation come those with yellow heads and gray hair, then those with white heads and gray hair, then those with golden wings covered with red hair, those of yellow color with blood-red hair who are said to have two tails in [the] form of sheep's horns, finally those yellow in color with pointed head and long abdomen and those supposed to be dressed in embroidered silk, gray in color and covered with red spots like fish-scales. The good fighters, according to Chinese experts, are recognized by their loud chirping, their big heads and necks, long legs, and broad bodies and backs.

The "Generals," as stated, receive a special diet before the contest, and are attended to with utmost care and great competence. Observations made for many centuries have developed a set of standard rules which are conscientiously followed. The trainers, for instance, are aware of the fact that extremes of temperature are injurious to the crickets. When they observe that the insects droop their tiny mustaches, they know that they are too warm, and endeavor to maintain for them an even temperature and exclude all draughts from them. Smoke is supposed to be detrimental to their health, and the rooms in which they are kept must be perfectly free form it. The experts also have a thorough understanding of their diseases, and have prescriptions at hand for their treatment and cure. If the crickets are sick from overeating, they are fed on a kind of red insect. If sickness arises from cold, they get mosquitoes; if from heat, shoots of the green pea are given them. A kind of butterfly known as "bamboo butterfly" is administered for difficulty in breathing. In a word, they are cared for like pet babies.

The tournaments take place in an open space, on a public square, or in a special house termed

Autumn Amusements. There are heavy-weight, middle and light-weight champions. The wranglers are always matched on equal terms according to size, weight, and color, and are carefully weighed on a pair of wee scales at the opening of each contest. A silk cover is spread over a table on which are placed the pottery jars containing the warring crickets. The jar is the arena in which the prize fight is staged. . . . As a rule, the two adversaries facing each other will first endeavor to flee, but the thick walls of the bowl or jar are set up as an invincible barrier to this attempt at desertion. Now the referee who is called "Army Commander" or "Director of the Battle" intercedes, announcing the contestants and reciting the history of their past performances, and spurs the two parties on to combat. For this purpose he avails himself of the tickler described above, and first stirs their heads and the ends of their tails, finally their large hind legs. The two opponents thus excited stretch out their antennae which the Chinese not inaptly designate "tweezers," and jump at each other's heads. The antennae or tentacles are their chief weapons. One of the belligerents will soon lose one of its horns, while the other may retort by tearing off one of the enemy's legs. The two combatants become more and more exasperated and fight each other mercilessly. The struggle usually ends in the death of one of them, and it occurs not infrequently that the more agile or stronger one pounces with its whole weight upon the body of its opponent, severing its head completely.

Cricket-fights in China have developed into a veritable passion. Bets are concluded, and large sums are wagered on the prospective champions. The stakes are in some cases very large, and at single matches held

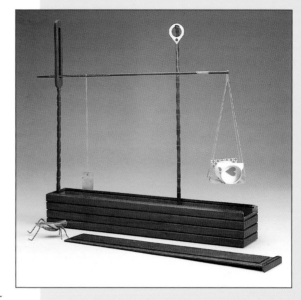

Cricket scale with wood storage box. Cricket weighing box made from playing cards. China, 20th century.

L' IMAGE ODIER–DANEE HAZAMA

Clay fighting arena with lid. 4¼" h. China, 20th century.

L' IMAGE ODIER–DANEE HAZAMA

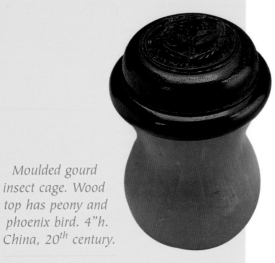

Moulded gourd insect cage. Wood top has peony and phoenix bird. 4"h. China, 20th century.

Moulded gourd insect cage with wire coil (huang). Ivory top has Chinese lion. 6"h. China, 20th century.

in Canton are said to have sometimes aggregated $100,000. It happens quite frequently that too ardent amateurs are completely ruined in the game. Gambling is forbidden by law in China as elsewhere, but such laws are usually winked at, and the official theory in this case is that the stakes consist of presents of sweet cakes. Choice champions fetch prices up to $100, the value of a good horse in China, and owners of famous crickets travel long distances to meet their competitors and congregate with them in order to match their champions. Some amateurs delight in raising them by the hundreds in the hope to produce the champion of the champions of the season, who is honored with the attribute of Grand Marshal. These men are by no means low-brows, but highly cultured men and those in responsible government positions are found in this class.

Two localities near Canton, Fa-ti and Cha-pi, not far from Whampoa, enjoy a special reputation for cricket fighting. At these places extensive mat sheds are erected and divided into several compartments. In each section a contest goes on, the pot which forms the arena being placed on a table. In order to acquaint prospective betters with the merits of the crickets matched against each other, a placard is posted on the sides of the building, setting forth various stakes previously won by each cricket. Great excitement is manifested at these matches, and considerable sums of money change hands. The sum of money staked on the contest is lodged with a committee who retain ten percent to cover expenses and hand over the balance to the owner of the winning cricket. The lucky winner is also presented with a roast pig, a piece of silk, and a gilded ornament resembling a bouquet of flowers. This decoration is deposited by him either on the ancestral altar of his house to inform his ancestors of his good luck and to thank them for their protection, or on a shrine in honor of Kwan-ti, a deified hero, who is the personification of all manly virtues and a model of gentlemanly conduct.

The names of the victorious champions are inscribed on an ivory tablet carved in the shape of a gourd (Plate 11, centre), and these tablets like diplomas are religiously kept in the houses of the fortunate owners. Sometimes the characters of the inscription are laid out in gold. The victory is occasion for great rejoicing and jollification. Music is performed, gongs are clanged, flags displayed, flowers scattered, and the tablet of victory is triumphantly marched in front, the jubilant victor struts in the procession of his overjoyed compatriots, carrying his victorious home. The sunshine of his glory falls on the whole community in which he lives, and his village will gain as much publicity and notoriety as an American town which has produced a golf or baseball champion.

In southern China, a cricket which has won many victories is honored with the title "conquering or victorious cricket" (*shou lip*); on its death it is placed in a small silver coffin, and is solemnly buried. The owner of the champion believes that the honorable interment will bring him good luck and that excellent fighting crickets will be found in the following year in the neighborhood of the place where his favorite cricket lies buried.

All these ideas emanate from the belief that able cricket champions are incarnations of great warriors and heroes of the past from whom they have inherited a soul imbued with prowess and fighting qualities. Dickens says, "For all the Cricket Tribe are potent Spirits, even though the people who hold converse with them do not know it (which is frequently the case)."

A proverbial saying with reference to a man who failed or has been defeated is, "A defeated cricket, –he gives up his mouth," which means as much as "throwing up the sponge."

PLATE II

BLUE AND WHITE PORCELAIN DISHES
FOR FEEDING CRICKETS.
In the centre an ivory tablet in shape of a gourd on which the names of the victorious champions are inscribed.

The History of the Chin Dynasty (*Chin shu*) mentions a fellow named Shan Tao-Khai who supposedly metamorphosed like a cicada by ingesting pills.

ricket Tales

THE FOLLOWING CHINESE STORIES may give an insight into the cricket rage. Kia Se-tao, a minister of state and general who lived in the thirteenth century, and who wrote, as mentioned, an authoritative treatise on the subject, is one of the cricket fanciers famous in history. He was completely obsessed with an all-absorbing passion for the cricket cult. The story goes that one day, during a war of the Mongols against the imperial house of Sung, an important city fell into the hands of the foe. When Kia Se-tao received news of the disaster, he was found kneeling in the grass of a lawn and taking part in a cricket match. "In this manner you look out for the interests of the nation!" he was reprimanded. He was not in the least disturbed, however, and kept his attention concentrated on the game.

An anecdote of tragical character is told with reference to an official of Peking, who held the post of director of the rice-granaries of the capital. He once found a cricket of choice quality and exceptional value. In order to secure this treasure, he exchanged his best horse for it and resolved to present this fine specimen to the emperor. He placed it cautiously in a box and took it home. During his absence his prying wife craved to see the insect which had been bought so dearly. She opened the box, and fate ordained that the cricket made its escape. A rooster happened to be around and swallowed the cricket. The poor woman, frightened by the consequences of her act, strangled herself with a rope. At his return the husband learned of the double loss he had suffered and, seized by despair, committed suicide. The Chinese narrator of the story concludes, "Who would have imagined that the graceful singer of the fields might provoke a tragedy like this?"

The *Strange Stories from a Chinese Studio* written by P'u Sung-ling in 1679 (translated into English by H.A. Giles) contains the following story of a Fighting Cricket (No.64):-

During the period Süan-te (1426-36) of the Ming dynasty, cricket fighting was very much in vogue at court (levies of crickets being exacted from the people as a tax.) On one occasion, the magistrate of Hua-yin, wishing to befriend the governor, presented him with a cricket which, on being set to fight, displayed very remarkable powers; so much so that the Governor commanded the magistrate to supply him regularly with these insects. The latter, in his turn, ordered the beadles of his district to provide him with crickets; and then it became a practice for people who had nothing else to do to catch and rear them for this purpose. Thus the price of crickets rose very high; and when the beadle's runners came to exact even a single one, it was enough to ruin

Oblong porcelain cricket jars with landscape and floral designs. 4"h. China, 19th century.

Ink painting on paper.
Boy and old man watching a
cricket fight. China.

several families. In the said village there lived a man named Cheng, a student who had often failed for his bachelor's degree; and, being a stupid sort of fellow, his name was sent in for the post of beadle. He did all he could to get out of it, but without success; and by the end of the year his small patrimony was gone. Just then came a call for crickets. Cheng was in despair, but, encouraged by his wife, went out hunting for the insects. At first he was unsuccessful, but by means of a map supplied by a fortune-teller he at last discovered a magnificent specimen, strong and handsome, with a fine tail, green neck, and golden wings; and, putting it in a basket, he returned home in high glee to receive the congratulations of his family. He would not have taken anything for this cricket, and proceeded to feed it carefully in a bowl. Its belly was the color of a crab's, its back that of a sweet chestnut; and Cheng tended it most lovingly, waiting for the time when the magistrate should call upon him for a cricket.

Meanwhile, Cheng's nine year old son, while his father was out, opened the bowl. The cricket escaped instantaneously. The boy grabbed it, seized one of its legs which broke off, and the little creature soon died. Cheng's wife turned deadly pale when her son, with tears in his eyes, told her what had happened. The boy ran away, crying bitterly. Soon after Cheng came home, and when he heard his wife's story, he felt as if he had been turned to ice. He went in search of his son whose body he discovered at the bottom of a well. The parents' anger thus changed into grief, but when they prepared to bury the boy, they found that he was still breathing. Toward the middle of the night he came to, but his reason had fled.

His father caught sight of the empty bowl in which he had kept the cricket, and at daybreak he suddenly heard the chirping of a cricket outside the house

*Clay insect jar. 2¾".
China, 19th century.*

43

door. Jumping up hurriedly, there was his lost insect; but, on trying to catch it, away it hopped directly. He chased it up and down, until finally it jumped into a corner of the wall; and then, looking carefully about, he espied it once more, no longer the same in appearance, but small and of a dark red color. Cheng stood looking at it, without trying to catch such a worthless specimen, when all of a sudden the little creature hopped into his sleeve; and, on examining it more closely, he noticed that it really was a handsome insect, with well-formed head and neck, and forthwith took it indoors.

He was now anxious to try its prowess; and it so happened that a young fellow of the village, who had a fine cricket which used to win every bout it fought, called on Cheng that very day. He laughed heartily at Cheng's champion, and producing his own, placed it side by side, to the great disadvantage of the former. Cheng's countenance fell, and he no longer wished to back his cricket. However, the young fellow urged him, and he thought that there was no use in rearing a feeble insect, and that he had better sacrifice it for a laugh; so they put them together in a bowl. The little cricket lay quite still like a piece of wood, at which the young fellow roared again, and louder than ever when it did not even move though tickled with a pig's bristle. By dint of tickling it was roused at last, and then it fell upon its adversary with such fury, that in a moment the young fellow's cricket would have been killed outright had not its master interfered and stopped the fight. The little cricket then stood up and chirped to Cheng as a sign of victory; and Cheng, overjoyed, was just talking over the battle with the young fellow, when a cock caught sight of the insect and ran up to catch it. Cheng was alarmed, but the cock luckily missed its aim, and the cricket hopped away, its enemy pursuing at full speed. In the next moment Cheng saw his cricket seated on the cock's head, holding firmly on to its comb. He then placed it in a cage and sent it to the magistrate, who, seeing what a small one he had provided, was very angry indeed. The magistrate refused to believe the story of the cock, so Cheng set it to fight with other crickets all of whom it vanquished without exception. He then tried it with a cock, and as all turned out as Cheng had said, he gave him a present and sent the cricket on to the Governor. The latter forwarded it to the palace in a golden cage with some comments on its performances.

It was found that in the splendid collection of his majesty there was not one worthy of being matched with this one. It would dance in time to music and became a great favorite at court. The emperor in return bestowed magnificent gifts of horses and silks upon the Governor. The latter rewarded the magistrate, and the magistrate recompensated Cheng by excusing him from the duties of beadle and by instructing the Literary Chancellor to pass him for the first degree. A few months afterwards Cheng's son recovered his intellect and said that he had been a cricket and had proved himself a very skillful fighter. The Governor also rewarded Cheng handsomely, and in a few years he was a rich man, with flocks, herds, houses and acres, quite one of the wealthiest of mankind."

The interesting point of this story is that the boy's spirit, during his period of temporary mental aberration, had entered into the body of the cricket which had allowed itself to be caught by his father. He animated it to fight with such extraordinary vigor that he might amend the loss caused by his curiosity in letting the other cricket escape.

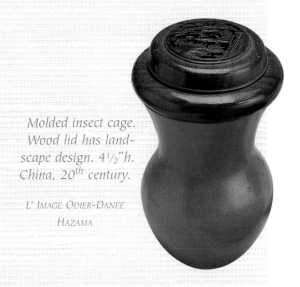

Molded insect cage. Wood lid has landscape design. 4½"h. China, 20th century.

L' IMAGE ODIER-DANEE
HAZAMA

PLATE 12

Carved Walnut Shell (Enlarged)
Decorated with the figures of the
Eighteen Arhat, a pavilion, trees,
and the sun emerging from the
clouds. For keeping singing
crickets and carried about in the
girdle. China, K'ien-lung Period
(1736-95).

Cricket-fights are not so cruel as cock and quail fights in which the Chinese also indulge, but the three combined are not so revolting as the bull-fights of Spain and Latin America. The Chinese reveal their sentimental qualities in their fondness of the insect-musicians, in the loving care they bestow on their pets and in lavishing on them the most delicate and exquisite productions their miniature art is able to create. They know how to carve a walnut-shell with the figures of the eighteen Arhat and elaborate ornamental detail (Plate 9 and 12). A lens is required to appreciate this whole apparatus of intricate design. A walnut like this is suspended at the girdle, and a cricket is enclosed in it just for the purpose of enjoying its musical efforts. Surely people who go to all this trouble must have sentiments and a deep sense of the joy of life and nature.

As far as I know, the Chinese are the only nation that has developed cricket-fights. The Japanese, though fond of chirping insects which they keep as pets in little cages, do not use them for fighting purposes. Kipling writes in his Jungle-book, "The herd-children of India sleep and wake and sleep again, and weave little baskets of dried grass and put grasshoppers in them; or catch two praying-mantises and make them fight." This may be an occasional occurrence in India, but it has not developed into a sport or a national pastime. . . .

Arthropods in the Arts

Insects have been a popular subject for Oriental artisans for centuries.

Crickets and cicadas appear in a variety of art forms including *netsuke*, *ojimi*, *enro*, *tsuba*, *cloisonné*, porcelain and pottery, snuff bottles, jade and weaving, painting, embroidery, carving, and casting.

During the reign of Emperor Tao Kuang (1821-1850), crickets were a popular decorative motif on snuff bottles.

The cicada adorns many ancient Shang and Zhou dynasty vessels.

Imperial painting books of ancient China included chapters on painting insects. Perhaps the best known painting book was *The Mustard Seed Garden Book of Painting*. It had a whole chapter devoted to insects.

When painting insects, it is important to be spontaneous so that the vitality of the insect is conveyed in the picture. The Mantis Body brush stroke used by Japanese painters attempted to capture the essence of insect life.

During the third century, Chinese painter Tsao Fu-shing painted a fly so realistic that the emperor tried to brush it off the painting.

Ceramic dish with insects and flowers. 4"h. China, 19th century.

L' IMAGE ODIER-DANEE HAZAMA

Ceramic vase with katydid and flowers. Wood top. 11½". China, 19th century.

L' IMAGE ODIER-DANEE HAZAMA

Glass snuff bottle with cricket. 2"h. China, 19th century.

L' IMAGE ODIER-DANEE HAZAMA

Two 18th-century painters Ba da shan ren, and Shi-tao, are well known for their abstract paintings of arthropods.

❋ ❋

Perhaps this century's best known Chinese insect painter is Qi Baishi (1863-1957). He painted insects from nature, unlike many painters who copied the works of other artists.

❋

Huang Ch'uan's 1887 book *Beautiful Birds from Life* has many examples of paintings containing insects.

❋

Other well-known Chinese insect painters:
Teng Changyu • Emperor Liang Yuandi
Lu Tanwei • Gu Junzhi
Xu Xi • Ma Quan • Yun Bing
Chai Zhenyi • Xue Susu

❋

METHOD OF PAINTING INSECTS AMONG HERBACEOUS PLANTS

When painting insects that live among herbaceous plants, attention should be given to rendering their appearance when flying, fluttering, chirping, or hopping. Flying, the wings of insects are unfurled; returnung to rest, folded again. Those that chirp vibrate parts of their forewings against their haunches, making the sharp sounds that are their song. Those that hop straighten their bodies, poised, as it were, on tiptoe, giving an impression of lively skipping. Bees, wasps, and butterflies have a pair of large wings and a pair of small. Insects that live among grasses have six pairs of long and short legs.
—FROM THE MUSTARD SEED GARDEN MANUAL OF PAINTING

Vase with insects and leaves. 12½"h.
China, 19th century.

L' IMAGE ODIER-DANEE HAZAMA

PART TWO
INSECT-MUSICIANS

Mushi yo mushi,

Naïté ingwa ga

Tsukuru nara?

"O insect, insect!— think you that Karma can be exhausted by song?"

—JAPANESE POEM.

I

IF YOU EVER VISIT JAPAN, be sure to go to at least one temple-festival, — *en-nichi*. The festival ought to be seen at night, when everything shows to the best advantage in the glow of countless lamps and lanterns. Until you have had this experience, you cannot know what Japan is, — you cannot imagine the real charm of queerness and prettiness, the wonderful blending of grotesquery and beauty, to be found in the life of the common people.

In such a night you will probably let yourself drift awhile with the stream of sightseers through dazzling lanes of booths full of toys indescribable — dainty puerilities, fragile astonishments, laughter-making oddities; — you will observe representations of demons, gods, and goblins; — you will be startled by *mandō* immense lantern-transparencies, with monstrous faces painted upon them; — you will have glimpses of jugglers, acrobats, sword-dancers, fortune-tellers; — you will hear everywhere, above the tumult of voices, a ceaseless blowing of flutes and booming of drums. All this may not be worth stopping for. But presently, I am almost sure, you will pause in your promenade to look at a booth illuminated like a magic-lantern, and stocked with tiny wooden cages out of which an incomparable shrilling proceeds. The booth is the booth of a vendor of singing-insects; and the storm of noise is made by the insects. The sight is curious; and a foreigner is nearly always attracted by it.

But having satisfied his momentary curiosity, the foreigner usually goes on his way with the idea that he has been inspecting nothing more remarkable than a particular variety of toys for children. He might easily be made to understand that the insect-trade of Tōkyō alone represents a yearly value of thousands of dollars; but he would certainly wonder if assured that the insects themselves are esteemed for the peculiar character of the sounds which they make. It would not be easy to convince him that in the aesthetic life of a most refined and artistic people, these insects hold a place not less important or well-deserved than that occupied in Western civilization by our thrushes, linnets, nightingales and canaries. What stranger could suppose that a literature one thousand years old, — a literature full of curious and delicate beauty, — exists upon the subject of these short-lived insect-pets?

The object of the present paper is, by elucidating these facts, to show how superficially our travelers might unconsciously judge the most interesting details of Japanese life. But such misjudgments are as natural as they are inevitable. Even with the kindest of intentions it is impossible to estimate correctly at sight anything of the extraordinary in Japanese custom, — because the extraordinary nearly always relates to feelings, beliefs, or thoughts about which a stranger cannot know anything.

Before proceeding further, let me observe that the domestic insects of which I am going to speak, are mostly night-singers, and must not be confounded with the *semi* (cicadae), mentioned in former essays of mine. I think that the cicadae, — even in a country so exceptionally rich as is Japan in musical insects, — are wonderful melodists in their own way. But the Japanese find as much difference between the notes of night-insects and of cicadae as we find between those of larks and sparrows; and they relegate their cicadae to the vulgar place of chatters. *Semi* are therefore never caged. The national liking for caged insects does not mean a liking for mere noise; and the note of every insect in public favor must possess either some rhythmic charm, or some mimetic quality celebrated in poetry or legend. The same fact is true of the Japanese liking for the chant of frogs. It would be a mistake to suppose that all kinds of frogs are considered musical; but there are particular species of very small frogs having sweet notes; and these are caged and petted.

Of course, in the proper meaning of the word, insects do not *sing*; but in the following pages I may occasionally employ the terms "singer" and "singing-insect," — partly because of their convenience, and partly because of their correspondence with the language used by Japanese insect-dealers and poets, describing the "voices" of such creatures.

II

THERE ARE MANY CURIOUS REFERENCES in the old Japanese classic literature to the custom of keeping musical insects. For example in the chapter entitled 'Nowaki'[1] of the famous novel *Genji Monogatari*, written in the latter part of the tenth century by the Lady Murasaki-Shikibu, it is stated: 'The maids were ordered to descend to the garden, and give some water to the insects.' But the first definite mention of cages for singing-insects would appear to be the following passage from a work entitled *Chomon-Shu*: —

'On the twelfth day of the eighth month of the second year of Kaho (1095 A.D.), the Emperor ordered his pages and chamberlains to go to Sagano and find some insects. The Emperor gave them a cage of network of bright purple thread. All, even the head-chaplain and his attendants, taking horses from the Right and the Left Imperial Mews, then went on horseback to hunt for insects. Tokinori Ben, at that time holding the office of *Kurando*[2], proposed to the party as they rode toward Sagano, a subject for poetical composition. The subject was, *Looking for insects in the fields*. On reaching Sagano, the party dismounted, and walked in various directions for a distance of something more than ten *chō*[3], and sent their attendants to catch the insects. In the evening they returned to the palace. They put into the cage some *hagi*[4] and *ominameshi* (for the insects). The cage was respectfully presented to the Empress. There was *saké*-drinking in the palace that evening; and many poems were composed. The Empress and her court-ladies joined in the making of the poems'.

This would appear to be the oldest Japanese record of an insect-hunt, — though the amusement may have been invented earlier than the period of Kaho. By the seventeenth century it seems to have become a popular diversion; and night-hunts were in vogue as much as day-hunts. In the *Teikoku Bunshū*, or collected works of the poet Teikoku, who died during the second year of Shōwō (1653), there has been preserved one of the poet's letters which contains a very interesting passage on the subject. 'Let us go insect-hunting this evening,' — writes the poet to his friend. 'It is true that the night will be very dark, since there is no moon; and it may seem dangerous to go out. But there are many people now going to the graveyards every night, because the Bon festival is approaching[5]; — therefore the way to the fields will not be lonesome for us. I have prepared many lanterns;— so the *hata-ori*, *matsumushi*, and other insects will probably come to the lanterns in great number.'

It would also seem that the trade of insect-seller (*mushiya*) existed in the seventeenth century; for in a diary of that time, known as the *Diary of Kikaku*, the writer speaks of his disappointment at not finding any insect-dealers in Yedo, — tolerably good evidence that he had met such persons elsewhere. 'On the thirteenth day of the sixth month of the fourth year of Teikyo (1687), I went out," he writes, "to look for *kirigirisu*-sellers. I searched for them in Yotsuya, in Kōjimachi, in Hongō, in Yushimasa, and in both divisions of Kanda-Sudamachō[6], but I found none.'

As we shall presently see, the *kirigirisu* was not sold in Tōkyō until about one hundred and twenty years later.

But long before it became the fashion to keep singing-insects, their music had been celebrated by poets as one of the aesthetic pleasures of the autumn. There are charming references to singing-insects in poetical collections made during the tenth century, and doubtless containing many compositions of a yet earlier period. And just as places famous for cherry, plum, or other blossoming trees, are still regularly visited every year by thousands and tens of thousands, merely for the delight of seeing the flowers in their seasons, — so in ancient times city-dwellers made autumn excursions to country-districts simply for the pleasure of hearing the chirruping choruses of crickets and of locusts, — the night singers especially. Centuries ago places were noted as pleasure-resorts solely because of this melodious attraction; — such were Musashino (now Tōkyō), Yatano in the province of Echizen, and Mano in the province of Ōmi. Somewhat later, probably, people discovered that each of the principal species of singing-insects haunted by preference some particular locality, where its peculiar chanting could be heard to the best advantage; and eventually no less than eleven places became famous throughout Japan for different kinds of insect-music.

The best places to hear the *matsumushi* were: —

    (1) Arashiyama, near Kyōtō, in the province of Yamashiro;

    (2) Sumiyoshi, in the province of Settsu;

    (3) Miyagino, in the province of Mutsu.

The best places to hear the *suzumushi* were: —

    (4) Kagura-ga-Oka, in Yamashiro;

    (5) Ogura-yama, in Yamashiro;

    (6) Suzuka-yama, in Isé;

    (7) Narumi, in Owari.

The best places to hear the *kirigirisu* were: —

    (8) Sagano, in Yamashiro;

    (9) Takeda-no-Sato, in Yamashiro;

    (10) Tatsuta-yama, in Yamato;

    (11) Ono-no-Shinowara, in Ōmi.

Afterwards, when the breeding and sale of singing-insects became a lucrative industry, the custom of going into the country to hear them gradually went out of fashion. But even to-day city-dwellers, when giving a party, will sometimes place cages of singing-insects among the garden-shrubbery, so that the guests may enjoy not only the music of the little creatures, but also those memories or sensations of rural peace which such music evokes.

III

THE REGULAR TRADE IN MUSICAL INSECTS is of comparatively modern origin. In Tōkyō its beginnings date back only to the Kwansei era (1789-1800), — at which period, however, the capital of the Shōgunate was still called Yedo. A complete history of business was recently placed in my hands, — a history partly compiled from old documents, and partly from traditions preserved in the families of several noted insect-merchants of the present day.

The founder of the Tōkyō trade was an itinerant food seller named Chūzō, originally from Echigo, who settled in the Kanda district of the city in the latter part of the eighteenth century. One day, while making his usual rounds, it occurred to him to capture a few of the *suzumushi* , or bell-insects, then very plentiful in the Negishi quarter, and to try the experiment of feeding them at home. They throve and made music in confinement; and several of Chūzō's neighbors, charmed by their melo-dious chirruping, asked to be supplied with *suzumushi* for a consideration. From the acci-dental beginning, the demand for *suzumushi* grew rapidly to such proportions that the food

seller at last decided to give up his former calling and to become an insect-seller.

Chūzō only caught and sold insects: he never imagined that it would be more profitable to breed them. But the fact was presently discovered by one of his customers, — a man named Kirayama, then in the service of the Lord Aoyama Shi-mod-zuké-no-Kami. Kiriyama had bought from Chūzō several *suzumushi*, which

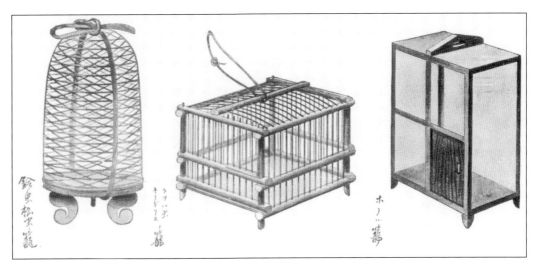

were kept and fed in a jar half-filled with moist clay. They died in the cold season; but during the following summer Kiriyama was agreeably surprised to find the jar newly peopled with a number of young ones, evidently born from eggs which the first prisoners had left in the clay. He fed them carefully, and soon had the pleasure, my chronicler says, of hearing them "begin to sing in small voices." Then he resolved to make some experiments; and, aided by Chūzō, who furnished the males and females, he succeeded in breeding not only *suzumushi*, but three other kinds of singing-insects also, — *kantan, matsumushi, and kutsuwamushi*. He discovered, at the same time, that, by keeping his jars in a warm room, the insects could be hatched consider-ably in advance of the natural season. Chūzō sold for Kiriyama these home-bred singers; and both men found the new undertaking profitable beyond expectation.

The example set by Kiriyama was imitated by a *tabiya*, or stocking-maker named Yasubei (commonly known as Tabiya Yasubei by reason of his calling), who lived in Kanda-ku. Yasubei likewise made careful study of the habits of singing-insects, with a view to their breeding and nourishment; and he soon found himself able to carry on a small trade in them. Up to that time the insects sold in Yedo would seem to have been kept in jars or boxes: Yasubei conceived the idea of having special cages manufactured for them. A man named Kondō, vassal to the Lord Kamei of Honjō-ku, interested himself in the matter, and made a number of pretty little cages which delighted Yasubei, and secured a large order from him. The new invention found public favor at once; and Kondō soon afterwards established the first manufactory of insect-cages.

The demand for singing-insects increased from this time so rapidly, that Chūzō soon found it impossible to supply all his would-be customers directly. He therefore decided to change his business to wholesale trade, and to sell to retail dealers only. To meet orders, he purchased largely from peasants in the suburbs and elsewhere. Many persons were employed by him; and Yasubei and others paid him a fixed annual sum for sundry rights and privileges.

Some time after this Yasubei became the first itinerant-vendor of singing-insects. He walked through the streets crying his wares; but hired a number of servants to carry the cages. Tradition says that while going his rounds he used to wear a *katabira* [7] made of a much-esteemed silk stuff called *sukiya*, together with fine a *Hakata*-girdle; and that this elegant way of dressing proved of much service to him in his business.

Two men, whose names have been preserved, soon entered into competition with Yasubei. The first was Yasakura Yasuzō, of Honjō-ku, by previous occupation a *sahainin*, or property-agent. He prospered, and became widely known as Mushi-Yasu, — "Yasu-the-Insect-Man." His success encouraged a former fellow — *sahainin*. Genbei of Uyeno, to go into the same trade. Genbei likewise found insect-selling a lucrative occupation, and earned for himself the sobriquet of Mushi-Gen, by which he is yet remembered. His descendants in Tōkyō to-day are *amé*-manufacturers; [8] but they still carry on the hereditary insect-business during the summer and autumn months; and one of the firm was kind enough to furnish me with many of the facts recorded in this little essay.

Chūzō, the father and founder of all this curious commerce, died without children; and sometime in the period of Bunsei (1818-1829) his business was taken over by a distant relative named Yamasaki Seïchirō. To Chūzō's business, Yamasaki joined his own, — that of a toy merchant. About the same time a law was passed limiting the number of insect-dealers in the municipality to thirty-six. The thirty-six then formed themselves into a guild, called the Ōyama-Kō ('Ōyama Society'), having for patron the divinity Sekison-Sama of the mountain Ōyama in Sagami Province.[9] But in business the association was known as the Yedō-Mushi-Kō, or Yedo Insect-Company.

It is not until after this consolidation of the trade that we hear of the *kirigirisu*, — the same musical insect which the poet Kikaku had vainly tried to buy in the city in 1687, — being sold in Yedo. One of the guild known as Mushiya Kojirō ('Kojirō the Insect-Merchant'), who did business in Honjō-Ku, returning to the city after a short visit to his native place in Kadzusa, brought back with him a number of *kirigirisu*, which he sold at a good profit. Although long famous elsewhere, these insects had never before been sold in Yedo.

'When Midzu Echizen-no-Kami,' says the chronicle, 'became *machi-bugyō* (or chief magistrate) of Yedo, the law limiting the number of insect-dealers to thirty-six, was abolished'. Whether the guild was subsequently dissolved the chronicle fails to mention.

Kiriyama, the first to breed singing-insects artificially, had, like Chūzō, built up a prosperous trade. He left a son, Kaméjirō, who was adopted into the family of one Yumoto, living in Waséda, Ushigomé-ku. Kaméjirō brought with him to the Yumoto family the valuable secrets of his father's occupation; and the Yumoto family is still celebrated in the business of insect breeding.

To-day the greatest insect-merchant in Tōkyō is said to be Kawasumi Kanésaburō, of Samon-cho in Yotsuya-ku. A majority of the lesser dealers obtain their autumn stock from him. But the insects bred artificially, and sold in the summer, are mostly furnished by the Yumoto house. Other noted dealers are Mushi-Sei, of Shitaya-ku, and Mushi-Toku, of Asakusa. These buy insects caught in the county, and brought to the city by the peasants. The wholesale dealers supply both insects and cages to multitudes of itinerant vendors who do business in the neighborhood of the parish-temples during the *en-nichi,* or religious festivals, — especially after dark. Almost every night of the year there are *en-nichi* in some quarter of the capital; and the insect-sellers are rarely idle during the summer and autumn months.

Perhaps the following list of current Tōkyō prices for singing-insects may interest the reader: —

> *Suzumushi*............3 sen 5 rin, to 4 sen
> *Matsumushi*..........4 "..................5"
> *Kantan*................10 "...............12"
> *Kin-hibari*............10 "...............12"
> *Kusa-hibari*...........10 "...............12"
> *Kuro-hibari*...........8 "...............12"
> *Kutsuwamushi*......10 "...............15"
> *Yamato-suzu*..........8 "...............12"
> *Kirigirisu*..............12 "...............15"
> *Emma-kōrogi*..........5 "
> *Kanétataki*..............12 "
> *Umaoi*....................10 "
> [Prices for the year 1897]

These prices, however, rule only during the busy period of the insect trade. In May and the latter part of June the prices are high, — for only artificially bred insects are then in the market. In July *kirigirisu* brought from the country will sell as low as one *sen*. The *kantan, kusa-hibari,* and *Yamato-suzu* sell sometimes as low as two *sen*. In August the *Emma-kōrogi* can be bought even at the rate of ten for one *sen*; and in September the *kuro-hibari, kanétataki,* and *umaoi* sell for one or one and a half *sen* each. But there is little variation at any season in the prices of *suzumushi* and of *matsumushi*. These are never very dear, but never sell at less than three *sen*; and there is always a demand for them. The *suzumushi* is the most popular of all; and the greater part of the profits annually made in the insect-trade is said to be gained on the sale of this insect.

IV

As will be seen from the foregoing price-list, twelve varieties of musical insects are sold in Tōkyō. Nine can be artificially bred, — namely the *suzu-mushi, matsumushi, kirigirisu, kantan, kutsuwamushi, Emma-kōrogi, kin-hibari, kusa-hibari* (also called *Asa-suzu*), and the *Yamato-suzu,* or *Yoshino-suzu.* Three varieties, I am told, are not bred for sale, but captured for the market: these are the *kanetataki, umaoi* or *hataori,* and *kuro-hibari.* But a considerable number of all the insects annually offered for sale, are caught in their native haunts.

The night-singers are, with few exceptions, easily taken. They are captured with the help of lanterns. Being quickly attracted by light, they approach the lanterns; and when near enough to be observed, they can readily be covered with nets or little baskets. Males and females are usually secured at the same time, for the creatures move about in couples. Only the males sing; but a certain number of females are always taken for breeding purposes. Males and females are kept in the same vessel only for breeding: they are never left together in a cage, because the male ceases to sing when thus mated, and will die in a short time after pairing.

The breeding pairs are kept in jars or other earthen vessels half-filled with moistened clay, and are supplied every day with fresh food. They do not live long: the male dies first, and the female survives only until her eggs have been laid. The young insects hatched from them, shed their skin in about forty days from birth, after which they grow more rapidly, and soon attain their full development. In their natural state these creatures are hatched a little before the *Doyō,* or Period of Greatest Heat by the old calendar, — that is to say, about the middle of July; — and they begin to sing in October. But when bred in a warm room, they are hatched early in April; and, with careful feeding, they can be offered for sale before the end of May. When very young, their food is triturated and spread for them upon a smooth piece of wood; but the adults are usually furnished with unprepared food, — consisting of parings of eggplant, melon-rind, cucumber-rind, or the soft interior parts of the white onion. Some insects, however, are specially nourished; — the *abura-kirigirisu,* for example, being fed with sugar-water and slices of musk-melon.

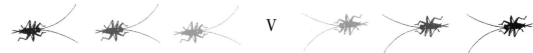

V

All the insects mentioned in the Tōkyō price-list are not of equal interest; and several of the names appear to refer only to different varieties of one species, — though on this point I am not positive. Some of the insects do not seem to have yet been scientifically classed; and I am no entomologist. But I can offer some general notes on the more important among the little melodists, and free translations of a few out of the countless poems about them, — beginning with the *matsumushi* which was celebrated in Japanese verse a thousand years ago:

MATSUMUSHI[10]

As ideographically written, the name of this creature signifies 'pine-insect;' but, as pronounced, it might mean also *'matsu,'* 'waiting-insect;' — since the verb *'matsu',* 'to wait,' and the noun *'matsu;'* 'pine,' have the same sound. It is chiefly upon this double meaning of the word as uttered that a host of Japanese poems about the *matsumushi* are based. Some of these are very old, — dating back to the tenth century at least.

Although by no means a rare insect, the *matsumushi* is much esteemed for the peculiar clearness and sweetness of its notes — (onomatopoetically rendered in Japanese by the syllables *chin-chirorin, chin-chirorin*), — little silvery shrillings which I can best describe as resembling the sound of an electric bell heard from a distance. The *matsumushi* haunts pine-woods and cryptomeria-groves, and makes its music at night. It is a very small insect, with a dark-brown back, and a yellowish belly.

Perhaps the oldest extant verses upon the *matsumushi* are those contained in the *Kokinshū,* — a famous anthology compiled in the year 905 by the court-poet Tsurayuki and several of his noble friends. Here we first find that play on the name of the insect as pronounced, which was to be repeated in a thousand different keys by a multitude of poets through the literature of more than nine hundred years: —

> *Aki no no ni*
> *Michi mo madoinu;*
> *Matsumushi no*
> *Koe sura kata ni*
> *Yadoya karamashi.*

"In the autumn-fields I lose my way; — perhaps I might ask for lodging in the direction of the cry of the waiting insect;" — that is to say, "might sleep to-night in the grass where the insects are waiting for me."

There is in the same work a much prettier poem on the *matsumushi* by Tsurayuki.

> *With dusk begins to cry the male of the Waiting-insect; — I, too, await*
> *my beloved, and, hearing, my longing grows.*

The following poems on the same insect are less ancient but not less interesting: —

> *Forever past and gone, the hour of the promised advent! — Truly the*
> *Waiter's voice is a voice of sadness now!*

> *Parting is sorrowful always, — even the parting with autumn!*
> *O plaintive matsumushi, add not thou to my pain!*

> *Always more clear and shrill, as the hush of the night grows deeper,*
> *The Waiting-insect's voice; — and I that wait in the garden,*
> *Feel enter into my heart the voice and the moon together.*

SUZUMUSHI[11]

The name signifies 'bell-insect;' but the bell of which the sound is thus referred to is a very small bell, or a bunch of little bells such as a Shintō priestess uses in the sacred dances. The *suzumushi* is a great favorite with insect-fanciers, and is bred in great numbers for the market. In the wild state it is found in many parts of Japan; and at night the noise made by multitudes of *suzumushi* in certain lonesome places might easily be mistaken, — as it has been by myself more than once, — for the sound of rapids. The Japanese description of the insect as resembling 'a watermelon seed' — the black kind — is excellent. It is very small, with a black back, and a white or yellowish belly. Its tintinnabulation —*ri-i-i-i-in*, as the Japanese render the sound — might easily be mistaken for the tinkling of a *suzu*. Both the *matsumushi* and the *suzumushi* are mentioned in Japanese poems of the period of Engi (901-922).

Some of the following poems on the *suzumushi* are very old; others are of comparatively recent date: —

> *Yes, my dwelling is old: weeds on the roof are growing;—*
> *But the voice of the suzumushi — that will never be old!*

> *To-day united in love, — we who can meet so rarely!*
> *Hear how the insects ring! — their bells to our hearts keeptime.*

> *The tinkle of tiny bells, — the voices of suzumushi,*
> *I hear in the autumn-dusk, — and think of the fields at home.*

> *Even the moonshine sleeps on the dews of the garden-grasses;*
> *Nothing moves in the night but the suzumushi's voice.*

> *Heard in these alien fields, the voice of the suzumushi, —*
> *Sweet in the evening-dusk, — sounds like the sound of home.*

> *Vainly the suzumushi exhausts its powers of pleasing,*
> *Always, the long night through, my tears continue to flow!*

> *Hark to those tinkling tones, — the chant of the suzumushi!*
> *— If a jewel of dew could sing, it would tinkle with such a voice!*

> *Foolish-fond I have grown; — I feel for the suzumushi! —*
> *In the time of the heavy rains, what will the creature do?*

HATAORI-MUSHI

The *hataori* is a beautiful bright-green grasshopper, of very graceful shape. Two reasons are given for its curious name, which signifies ' the Weaver.' One is that, when held in a particular way, the struggling gestures of the creature resemble the movements of a girl weaving. The other reason is that its music seems to imitate the sound of the reed and the shuttle of a hand-loom in operation, — *Ji-i-i-i* — *chon-chon!* — *ji-i-i-i*— *chon-chon!*

There is a pretty folk-story about the origin of the *hataori* and the *kirigirisu*, which used to be told to Japanese children in former times. — Long, long ago, says the tale, there were two very dutiful daughters who supported their old blind father by the labor of their hands. The elder girl used to weave, and the younger to sew. When the old blind father died at last, these good girls grieved so much that they soon died also. One beautiful morning, some creatures of a kind never seen before were found making music above the graves of the sisters. On the tomb of the elder was a pretty green insect, producing sounds like those made by a girl weaving, — ji-ï-ï-ï, *chon-chon! ji-ï-ï-ï, chon-chon!* This was the first *hataori-mushi*. On the tomb of the younger sister was an insect which kept crying out, '*Tsuzuré — sasé sasé ! — tsuzuré tsuzuré sasé, sasé, sasé!* ' (Torn clothes — patch, patch them up! — torn clothes, torn clothes — patch up, patch up, patch up!) This was the first *kirigirisu*. Then everybody knew that the spirits of the good sisters had taken those shapes. Still every autumn they cry to wives and daughters to work well at the loom, and warn them to repair the winter garments of the household before the coming of the cold.

Such poems as I have been able to obtain about the *hataori* consist of nothing more than pretty fancies. Two, of which I offer free renderings, are ancient, — the first by Tsurayuki; the second by a poetess classically known as 'Akinaka's Daughter': —

Weaving-insects I hear; and the fields, in their autumn-colors,
Seem of Chinese-brocade: — was this the weavers' work?

Gossamer-threads are spread over the shrubs and grasses:
Weaving-insects I hear; — do they weave with spider-silk?

UMAOI

The *umaoi* is sometimes confounded with the *hataori*, which it much resembles. But the true *umaoi* — (called *junta* in Izumo) — is a shorter and thicker insect than the *hataori*; and has at its tail a hook-shaped protuberance, which the weaver-insect has not. Moreover, there is some difference in the sounds made by the two creatures. The music of the *umaoi* is not '*ji-ï-ï-ï, —chon-chon*,' but, '*zu-ï-in-tzo! — zu-ï-in-tzō!*' — say the Japanese.

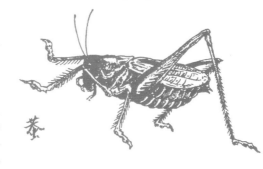

KIRIGIRISU[12]

There are different varieties of this much-prized insect. The *abura-kirigirisu*, a day-singer, is a delicate creature, and must be carefully nourished in confinement. The *tachi-kirigirisu*, a night-singer, is more commonly found in the market. Captured *kirigirisu* sold in Tōkyō are mostly from the neighborhood of Itabashi, Niiso, and Todogawa; and these, which fetch high prices, are considered the best. They are large vigorous insects, uttering very clear notes. From Kujiukuri in Kadzusa other and much cheaper *kirigirisu* are brought to the capital; but these have a disagreeable odor, suffer from the attacks of a peculiar parasite, and are feeble musicians.

As stated elsewhere, the sounds made by the *kirigirisu* are said to resemble those of the Japanese words, '*Tsuzuré — sasé! sasé!*' (Torn clothes — patch up! patch up!); and a large proportion of the many poems written about the insect depend for interest upon ingenious but untranslatable allusions to those words. I offer renderings therefore of only two poems on the *kirigirisu*, — the first by an unknown poet in the *Kokinshū*; the second by Tadafusa:—

O Kirigirisu! when the clover changes color,
Are the nights then sad for you as for me that cannot sleep?

O Kirigirisu! cry not, I pray, so loudly!
Hearing, my sorrow grows, — and the autumn-night is long!

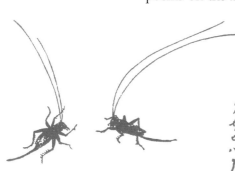

KUSA-HIBARI

The *kusa-hibari*, or 'Grass-Lark,'— also called *Asa-suzu*, or 'Morning-Bell;' *Yabu-suzu*, or 'the Little Bell of the Bamboo-grove;' *Aki-kazé* or 'Autumn-Wind;' and *Ko-suzu-mushi* 'or the Child of the Bell-Insect'— is a day-singer. It is very small, — perhaps the smallest of the insect-choir, except the *Yamato-suzu*.

KIN-HIBARI

The *kin-hibari*, or 'Golden Lark' used to be found in great numbers about the neighborhood of the well-known Shino-bazu-no-iké, — the great lotos-pond of Uyeno in Tōkyō; — but of late years it has become scarce there. The *kin-hibari* now sold in the capital are brought from Todogawa and Shimura.

KURO-HIBARI

The *kuro-hibari*, or 'Black Lark,' is rather uncommon, and comparatively dear. It is caught in the country about Tōkyō, but is never bred.

KOROGI

There are many varieties of this night-cricket, — called *kōrogi* from its music: — 'kiri-kiri-kiri-kiri! — kōro-kōro-kōro-kōro! — ghi-ï-ï-ï-ï-ï!' One variety, the *ebi-koro-gi*, or 'shrimp-kōrogi,' does not make any sound. But the *uma-kōrogi*, or 'horse-kōrogi;' the *Oni-kōrogi*, or 'Demon-kōrogi,' and the *Emma-kōrogi*, or 'Cricket-of-

エンマコヲロギ

Emma[13] [King of the Dead];'are all good musicians. The color is black-ish-brown, or black; — the best singing-varieties have curious wavy markings on the wings.

An interesting fact regarding the *korogi* is that mention of it is made in the very oldest collection of Japanese poems known, — the *Manyōshu*, probably compiled about the middle of the eighth century. The following lines, by an unknown poet, which contain this mention, are therefore considerably more than eleven hundred years old: —

Niwa-kusa ni
Murasame furite
Kōrogi no
Naku oto kikeba
Aki tsukinikeri.

['Showers have sprinkled the garden-grass. Hearing the sound of the crying of the *korogi*, I know that the autumn has come.']

エンマコヲロギ

KUTSUWAMUSHI.

There are several varieties of this extraordinary creature, — also called onomatopoetically *gatcha-gatcha.* — which is most provokingly described in dictionaries as 'a kind of noisy cricket' ! The variety commonly sold in Tōkyō has a green back, and a yellowish-white abdomen; but there are also brown and reddish varieties. The *kutsuwamushi* is difficult to capture, but easy to breed. As the *tsuku-tsuku-boshi* is the most wonderful musician among the sun-loving cicadae or *semi*, so the *kutsuwamushi* is the most wonderful of night-crickets. It owes its name, which means 'The Bridle-bit-Insect,' to its noise, which resembles the jingling and ringing of the old-fashioned Japanese bridle-bit (*kutsuwa*). But the sound is really much louder and much more complicated than ever was the jingling of a single *kutsuwa*; and the accuracy of the comparison is not easily discerned while the creature is storming beside you. Without the evidence of one's own eyes, it were hard to believe that so small a life could make so prodigious a noise. Certainly the vibratory apparatus in this insect must be very complicated. The sound begins with a thin sharp whizzing, as of leaking steam, and slowly strengthens; — then to the whizzing is suddenly

紡績娘

added a quick dry clatter, as of castanets; — and then, as the whole machinery rushes into operation, you hear, high above the whizzing and the clatter, a torrent of rapid ringing tones like the tapping of a gong. These, the last to begin, are also the first to cease; then the castanets stop; and finally the whizzing dies; — but the full orchestra may remain in operation for several hours at a time, without a pause. Heard from far away at night the sound is pleasant, and is really so much like the ringing of a bridle-bit, that when you first listen to it you cannot but feel how much real poetry belongs to the name of this insect, — celebrated from of old as 'playing at ghostly escort in ways where no man can pass.'

The most ancient poem on the *kutsuwamushi* is perhaps the following, by the Lady Idzumi-Shikibu: —

> *Waga seko wa*
> *Koma ni makasété*
> *Kinikeri to,*
> *Kiku ni kikasuru*
> *Kutsuwamushi kana!*

— which might be thus freely rendered:

> *Listen! — his bridle rings; — that is surely my husband*
> *Homeward hurrying now — fast as the horse can bear him! ...*
> *Ah! my ear was deceived! — only the Kutsuwamushi!*

KANTAN

This insect — also called *kantan-gisu*, and *kantan-no-kirigirisu*, — is a dark-brown night-cricket. Its note —"zi-ï-ï-ï-ïn" — is peculiar: I can only compare it to the prolonged twang of a bow-string. But this comparison is not satisfactory, because there is a penetrant metallic quality in the twang, impossible to describe.

VI

BESIDES POEMS ABOUT THE CHANTING OF PARTICULAR INSECTS, there are countless Japanese poems, ancient and modern, upon the voices of night-insects in general, — chiefly in relation to the autumn season. Out of a multitude I have selected and translated a few of the more famous only, as typical of the sentiment or fancy of hundreds. Although some of my renderings are far from literal as to language, I believe that they express with tolerable faithfulness the thought and feeling of the originals: —

> *Not for my sake alone, I know, is the autumn's coming; —*
> *Yet, hearing the insects sing, at once my heart grows sad.*

KOKINSHU.

Faint in the moonshine sounds the chorus of insect-voices:
To-night the sadness of autumn speaks in their plaintive tone.

I never can find repose in the chilly nights of autumn,
Because of the pain I hear in the insects' plaintive song.

How must it be in the fields where the dews are falling thickly!
In the insect-voices that reach me I hear the tingling of cold.

Never I dare to take my way through the grass in autumn:
Should I tread upon insect-voices[14] — what would my feelings be!

The song is ever the same, but the tones of the insects differ,
Maybe their sorrows vary, according to their hearts

Idzumi-Shikibu.

Changed is my childhood's home — all but those insect-voices:
I think they are trying to speak of happier days that were.

These trembling dews on the grass — are they tears for the death of
autumn? — Tears of the insect-singers that now so sadly cry?

It might be thought that several of the poems above given were intended to express either real or an affected sympathy with imagined insect-pain. But this would be a wrong interpretation. In most compositions of this class, the artistic purpose is to suggest, by indirect means, various phases of the emotion of love, — especially that melancholy which lends its own passional tone to the aspects and the voices of nature. The baroque fancy that dew might be insect-tears, is by its very exaggeration intended to indicate the extravagance of grief, as well as to suggest that human tears have been freshly shed. The verses in which a woman declares that her heart has become too affectionate, since she cannot but feel for the bell-insect during a heavy shower, really bespeak the fond anxiety felt for some absent beloved, traveling in the time of the great rains. Again, in the lines about 'treading on insect-voices', the dainty scruple is uttered only as a hint of that intensification of feminine tenderness which love creates. And a still more remarkable example of this indirect double-suggestiveness is offered by the little poem prefacing this article, —

"O insect, insect! — think you that Karma can be exhausted by song?"

The Western reader would probably suppose that the insect-condition, or insect-state-of-being, is here referred to; but the real thought of the speaker, presumably a woman, is that her own sorrow is the result of faults committed in former lives, and is therefore impossible to alleviate.

It will have been observed that a majority of the verses cited refer to autumn and to the sensations of autumn. Certainly Japanese poets have not been insensible to the real melancholy inspired by autumn, — that vague strange annual revival of ancestral pain: dim inherited sorrow of millions of memories associated through millions of years with the death of summer; — but in nearly every utterance of this melancholy, the veritable allusion is to grief of parting. With its color-changes, its leaf-whirlings, and the ghostly plaint of its insect-voices, autumn Buddhistically symbolizes impermanency, the certainty of bereavement, the pain that clings to all desire, and the sadness of isolation.

But even if these poems on insects were primarily intended to shadow amorous emotion, do they not reflect also for us the subtlest influences of nature, — wild pure nature, — upon imagination and memory? Does not the place accorded to insect-melody, in the home-life as well as in the literature of Japan, prove an aesthetic sensibility developed in directions that yet remain for us almost unexplored? Does not the shrilling booth of the insect-seller at a night-festival proclaim even a popular and universal comprehension of things divined in the West only by our rarest poets: — the pleasure-pain of autumn's beauty, the weird sweetness of the voices of the night, the magical quickening of remembrance by echoes of forest and field? Surely we have something to learn from the people in whose mind the simple chant of a cricket can awaken whole fairy-swarms of tender and delicate fancies. We may boast of being their masters in the mechanical, — their teachers of the artificial in all its varieties of ugliness; — but in the knowledge of the natural, — in the feeling of the joy and beauty of earth, — they exceed us like the Greeks of old. Yet perhaps it will be only when our blind aggressive industrialism has wasted and sterilized their paradise, — substituting everywhere for beauty the utilitarian, the conventional, the vulgar, the utterly hideous, — that we shall begin with remorseful amazement to comprehend the charm of that which we destroyed.

NOTES

1. Nowaki is the name given to certain destructive storms usually occuring toward the end of autumn. All the chapters of the *Genji Monogatari* have remarkably poetical and effective titles. There is an English translation, by Mr. Kencho Suyematsu, of the first seventeen chapters. [See also *The Tale of Genji*. Translated by Arthur Waley. New York: Random House, 1960.]

2. The Kurando, or Kurodo, was an official intrusted with the care of the imperial records.

3. A *cho* is about one-fifteenth of a mile.

4. *Hagi* is the name commonly given to bush-clover. *Ominameshi* is the common term for the *Valeriana officinalis*.

5. That is to say, there are now many people who go every night to the graveyards, to decorate and prepare the graves before the great Festival of the Dead.

6. Most of these names survive in the appellations of well-known districts of the present Tokyo.

7. Katabira is a name given to many kinds of light textures used for summer-robes. The material is usually hemp, but sometimes, as in the case referred to here, of fine silk. Some of these robes are transparent, and very beautiful. Hakata, in Kyushu, is still famous for the silk girdles made there. The fabric is very heavy and strong.

8. *Amé* is a nutritive gelatinous extract obtained from wheat and other substances. It is sold in many forms - as candy, as a syrupy liquid resembling molasses, as a sweet hot drink, as a solid jelly. Children are very fond of it. Its principle element is starch-sugar.

9. Oyama mountain in Sagami is a great resort of pilgrims. There is a celebrated temple there, dedicated to Iwanaga-Himé ('Long-Rock Princess'), sister of the beautiful Goddess of Fuji. Sekison-San is a popular name both for the divinity and for the mountain itself.

10. Calyptotryphus marmoratus (?).

11. Homeogryllus japonicus.

12. Locusta japonica (?).

13. In Sanskrit *Yama*. Probably this name was given to the insect on account of its large staring eyes. Images of King Emma are always made with very big and awful eyes.

14. *Mushi no koe fumu.*

COMMON SINGING INSECTS & FIGHTING CRICKETS OF CHINA

Grylloidea	Colloquial Name	English Meaning
Anaxipha pallidula	*xiao huang ling*	small yellow bell
Anaxipha sp.	*da huang ling*	large yellow bell
Homeoxipha lycoides	*mo ling*	inky bell
Svistellabifasciatata	*jin ling zi*	golden bell
Dianemobius fascipes	*ban ling*	spotted bell
Dianemobius flavoantennalis	*hua ling*	flowered bell
Ornebius kanetataki	*shi ling*	stony bell
Scleropterus punctatus	*pan ling*	rocky bell
Oecanthus longicaudus	*zhu ling*	bamboo bell
Homoeogryllus japonica	*ma ling*	horse bell
Truljaliahibinonis	*jin zhong*	golden bell
Truljalia forceps	*jin zhong*	golden bell
Xenogryllus marmoratus	*bao ta ling*	pagoda bell
Turanogryllus eous	*qing ling*	blue bell
Gryllodes sigillatus	*zhao ji*	stove chick
Velarifictorus micado	*cu zhi*	fighting cricket
Velarifictorus aspersus	*cu zhi*	fighting cricket
Gryllus bimaculatus	*hua jing*	painted mirror
Teleogryllus emma	*you hu lu*	oil gourd
Loxoblemmus doenitzi	*guan cai tou*	coffin-headed cricket
Tarbinskiellus portentosus	*da xi shuai*	giant cricket

Tettigonioidea

Mecopodaelongata	*fang zhi niang*	weaving lady
Gampsocleis gratiosa	*jiao ge-ge*	singing brother
Gampsocleis sadakovii obscura	*jiao ge-ge*	singing brother
Uvarovites inflatus	*jie er*	singing insect
Hexacentrus unicolor	*xiao fang zhi niang*	small weaving lady
Conocephalus maculatus	*cao zhong*	grass katydid
Conocephalus melas	*cao zhong*	grass katydid
Ruspolia lineosa	*cao zhong*	grass katydid
Ducetiajaponica	*lu zhong*	wing exposed katydid

COMMON SINGING INSECTS OF JAPAN

Colloquial Name	English Meaning
semi	cicada
suzumushi	bell-insect
matsumushi	pine insect, waiting insect
kantan(kantan-gisu or kantan-no-kirigirisu)	Kantan cricket
kin-hibari	golden-lark
kusa-hibari	grass-lark
asa-suzu	morning-bell
yabu-suzu	the little bell of the bamboo grove
aki-kazé	autumn-wind
ko-suzu-mushi	child of the bell insect
kuro-hibari	black-lark
kutsuwamushi	the bridle-bit-insect
Yamato-suzu	Yamato-bell
Yoshino-suzu	Yoshino-bell
kirigirisu	cricket
abura-kirigirisu	oil-cricket
tachi-kirigirisu	sword-cricket
kōrogi	cricket
ebi-kōrogi	shrimp-cricket
Emma-kōrogi	cricket of Emma
uma-kōrogi	horse-cricket
oni-kōrogi	large demon-cricket
kanétataki	bell-ringer
hataori-mushi	the weaver [weaver-insect]

Major Dynasties of China & Japan

China

Shang dynasty 1523-1028 B.C.
Chou (Zhou) dynasty 1027-256 B.C.
Ch'in (Qin) dynasty 221-206 B.C.
Han dynasty A.D. 206-220
Six dynasties 220-589
Sui 581-618
T'ang (Tang) 618-906
Five dynasties 907-960
Sung (Song) dynasty 960-1278
Yuan dynasty 1280-1368
Ming dynasty 1368-1643
Ch'ing (Qing) dynasty 1644-1912
Republic of China 1912-
People's Republic of China 1949-

Japan

Jomon period ca. 10,000-ca. 200 B.C.
Yayoi period ca. 200 B.C.-ca. A.D. 200
Tumulus (Kofun) period 200 -552
Asuka period 552-645
Nara period 645-794
Heian period 794-1185
Kamakura period 1185-1333
Muromachi (Ashikaga) period 1333-1573
Momoyama period 1573-1614
Edo (Tokugawa) period 1614-1868
Meiji period 1868-1911
Taisho 1912-1926
Showa period 1926-

Note: Pinyin spellings appear in parenthesis.

SOURCES

Here is a select list of resources used in this book. There are a number of Asian art societies and ento-mological associations that can provide more information. Their addresses can be found at the library.

CONTEMPORARY INSECT CAGES

J'Aimee Products
2253 Linda Avenue
Saginaw, MI 48603-4120
Phone: 517-790-9195
  Rectangular wood cage with glass front. Includes plastic feeding dishes, food packet and informational pamphlet.

Tierney Specialties
1021 El Camino Avenue
Stockton, CA 95209
Phone: 209-477-8271
Fax: 209-957-2847
  Screen cage with metal top and base.

GOURDS FOR CAGE MAKING

The Gourd Factory
P.O. Box 9
Linden, CA 95236
Phone: 209-887-3694
Fax: 209-887-2856
  Gourd growers. Mail order, wholesale and retail.

ANTIQUE INSECT CAGES

Patsy Donegan Antiques
Baker Hamilton Square
700 7th Street
Suite 106
San Francisco, CA 94107
Phone: 415-621-1624
  Asian antiques and folk art. Specializing in Chinese cricket cages, bird cages and paraphernalia.

Far East Godown
151 W. South Street
Boulder Creek, CA 95006
Phone: 408-338-9277
Fax: 408-338-3666
  Antique and contemporary insect cages. Cages are shown at *Collective Antiques*, 55 E. Third Street, San Mateo, CA.

Alex Cheung Co.
938 Chung King Road
Los Angeles, CA 90012
Phone: 213-629-4705
Fax: 213-680-0239
  Chinese antiques and art. Contemporary and antique insect cages.

CRICKETS

Crickets are available at many pet shops and bait & tackle stores or you can order them by mail order.

Bassetts Cricket Ranch, Inc.
365 S. Mariposa
Visalia, CA 93292
Phone: 800-634-2445
Fax: 209-747-3619
  Live crickets through the mail.

ASSOCIATIONS

The Young Entomologists' Society
1915 Peggy Place
Lansing, MI 48910

Entomological Society of Canada
393 Winston Avenue
Ottawa, Ontario
Canada V2A 1Y8

MUSEUMS WITH INSECT CAGE COLLECTIONS

Buffalo Museum of Science
1020 Humbolt Parkway
Buffalo, NY 14211

The Field Museum
1200 South Lakeshore Drive
Chicago, IL 60605

MUSEUMS WITH INSECT COLLECTIONS

American Museum of Natural History
Central Park West at
79th Street
New York, NY 10024

The Carnegie Museum of Natural History
4400 Forbes Avenue
Pittsburgh, PA 15213

The Denver Museum of Natural History
2001 Colorado Blvd.
Denver, CO 80205

Houston Museum of Natural Science
1 Hermann Circle Drive
Houston, TX 77030

Liberty Science Center
251 Philip Street
Jersey City, NJ 07305

Natural History Museum of Los Angeles County
900 Exposition Blvd.
Los Angeles, CA 90007

Royal Ontario Museum
Department of Entomology
100 Queens Park
Toronto, Ontario
Canada M5S 2C6

PHOTO: CLINT SHAW

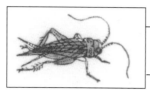

GLOSSARY

Antenna (*pl.* antennae) An appendage on an insect's head sometimes called a "feeler".

Arthropod A member of the Arthropoda phylum of segmented invertebrates.

Benjiao The chirping sound of an insect with unwaxed wings.

Benzhang A naturally shaped, unmolded gourd.

Chafan A gourd with a turn (*fan*) larger than its belly (*du*).

Cicada (*pl.* cicadae) An insect that produces a sound by vibrating membranes on its abdomen.

Class A subdivision of a phylum.

Cricket An insect of the Orthoptera order.

Dian yiao (*zhan yiao*) The process of waxing an insects wings for the purpose of amplifying its chirping sound.

Diandi The soil mixture placed in the bottom of gourds for ground dwelling insects.

Diyao The wax applied to an insects bottom wing.

Entomology The study of insects.

Family A subdivision of an order.

Fen The process of raising insects.

Gaiyao The wax applied to the top wing of an insect.

Genera (*pl.* genus) A subdivision of a family.

Gourd A fruit related to squash and pumpkins.

Guan muzi A gourd or a mold made for the palace or aristocracy.

Guanjia An insect breeder (literally means "jar man" because insects used to be bred in jars).

Hai'ercha An herbal tea added to *diandi*.

Hefeng An insect with loose wings.

Huang A spiral coil placed in an insect cage.

Jiaodeng An annual festival where people go to listen to their insects chirp.

Kuifan A gourd with a turn (*fan*) smaller than its belly (*du*).

Làbang The short, quick chirps made by a young cricket.

Làbang Sagging wings.

Lianbang The continuous chirping of an adult cricket.

Mushiya An insect-seller.

Muzi hulu A moulded gourd.

Order A subdivision of a class.

Orthoptera An order of insects.

Ovipositor An organ used for depositing eggs. On the cricket it is a spine shaped organ on the rear end of the female's abdomen.

Palabang Sagging wings.

Shou lip The victorious cricket in a cricket fighting match.

Stridulate To make sound by rubbing together parts of the body.

Tao A drawstring bag used to hold an insect cage.

Phylum A primary division of the animal kingdom.

Yanbo A long necked gourd.

Yazi The process of suppressing eggs by controlling the heat and humidity.

Ziguan A jar used to raise insects.

SELECTED BIBLIOGRAPHY

Aston, W.G. *Nihongi: Chronicles of Japan from the Earliest Times to A.D. 697.* Tokyo: Charles E. Tuttle Company, 1972.

Berenbaum, May R. *Bugs in the System: Insects and Their Impact on Human Affairs.* New York: Addison-Wesley, 1995.

Berliner, N.Z. *Chinese Folk Art: The Small Skills of Carving Insects.* Boston: Little, Brown and Company, 1986.

Betchaku, Y. and J.B. Mirviss. *Utamaro: Songs of the Garden.* New York: Viking Press, 1984.

Brand, J. *Observations on the Popular Antiquities of Great Britain,* vol. 3. 1888. p. 189 (n.p.)

Chai, Ch'u and Winberg Chai. ed. and trans. *A Treasury of Chinese Literature: A New Prose Anthology Including Fiction and Drama.* New York: Thomas Y. Crowell Company, 1974.
This anthology includes a cricket story.

Cohn, Don J. editor. *Vignettes From the Chinese: Lithographs from Shanghai in the Late Nineteenth Century.* Hong Kong: The Research Centre of Translation, The Chinese University of Hong Kong, 1987.
Stories from old Chinese newspapers including one about crickets and several about other insects. Illustrated.

Dethier, Vincent. *Crickets and Katydids, Concerts and Solos.* Cambridge: Harvard University Press, 1992.
Introduction to crickets and katydids in the North Eastern United States.

Edelstein, Debra. *Views From Jade Terrace: Chinese Women Artists 1300-1912.* Indianapolis and New York: Indianapolis Museum of Art and Rizzoli International Publications, Inc., 1988.
This book includes several insect paintings.

Hammond, Carol. "The Courtly Crickets". *Arts of Asia,* (March-April, 1983): 81-87.

Hearn, Lafcadio. "Insect-Musicians." In *Exotics and Retrospectives.* Boston: Little, Brown and Company, 1898.

Hucker, Charles O. *China's Imperial Past: An Introduction to Chinese History and Culture.* Stanford: Stanford University Press, 1975.

Laufer, Berthold. *Insect Musicians and Cricket Champions of China.* Leaflet 22. Chicago: Field Museum of Natural History, 1927.

Lutz, Frank E. "Insect Sounds". *Natural History,* (No. 2, 1926)

Mai-Mai, Sze. *The Way of Chinese Painting: Its Ideas and Technique.* New York: Random House, 1959.
Informative chapter on insect painting technique.

Nehring, Nancy. "Setting Up Your Own Cricket Colony". *Reptiles,* (July 1995): 24-26.
Good overview of how to breed crickets.

Pu, Songling. *Strange Tales From Make-Do Studio.* Edited by Denis C. and Victor H. Mair. Beijing: Foreign Languages Press, 1989.

Sei, Shonagon. *The Pillow Book Of Sei Shanogon.* Translated and edited by Ivan Morris. Baltimore: Penguin Books, 1967.

Shikibu, Murasaki. *The Tale of Genji.* Translated by Arthur Waley. New York: Random House, 1960.

Soloman, Barry. "The Cricket Story". *Arts of Asia,* (Nov. - Dec. 1983): 76-87.

Stilwell, Alison. *Chin Ling: The Chinese Cricket.* Carmel: The Stilwell Studio, 1981.
Children's book about pet crickets in China.

Wang, Shixiang. *The Charms of the Gourd.* Edited by the Editorial Committee of Next Magazine, Translated by Hu Shiping. Hong Kong: Next Publication, Ltd., 1993.
Comprehensive study of gourds including gourd insect cages.

INDEX